W9-AJS-936

Careers in Focus

COMPUTER & VIDEO GAME DESIGN

Ferguson
An imprint of ☑® Facts On File

Careers in Focus: Computer & Video Game Design

Copyright © 2005 by Facts On File, Inc.

Ferguson
An imprint of Facts On File, Inc.
132 West 31st Street
New York NY 10001

Library of Congress Cataloging-in-Publication Data
Careers in focus. Computer and video game design.
    p. cm.
    Includes index.
    ISBN 0-8160-5850-4 (hc : alk. paper)
    1. Computer games—Programming—Vocational guidance—Juvenile literature.
2. Video games—Design—Vocational guidance—Juvenile literature. I. Title:
Computer and video game design.
    QA76.76.C672C33 2005
    794.8'1526—cd22

Ferguson books are available at special discounts when purchased in bulk
quantities for businesses, associations, institutions, or sales promotions.
Please call our Special Sales Department in New York at (212) 967-8800 or
(800) 322-8755.

You can find Ferguson on the World Wide Web at http://www.fergpubco.com

Text design by David Strelecky

Printed in the United States of America

MP JT 10 9 8 7 6 5 4 3 2 1

This book is printed on acid-free paper.

Table of Contents

Introduction

Careers in Focus: Computer & Video Game Design describes a variety of careers in the computer and video game industry—at game companies, animation studios, law firms, marketing research firms, recording studios, retail stores, and publishing companies. These careers are as diverse in nature as they are in their earnings and educational requirements. Earnings range from minimum wage for entry-level software store employees to $200,000 or more for intellectual property lawyers and top designers. A few of these careers—such as software store employees—require little formal education but are excellent starting points for a career in the industry. Other jobs, such as sound workers and webmasters, require some postsecondary training or an associate's degree. Many positions in this industry (such as artists and animators, computer programmers, and computer and video game designers) require a minimum of a bachelor's degree. The career of intellectual property lawyer requires a law degree.

According to the Entertainment Software Association, the U.S. computer and video game industry had sales of $7 billion in 2003—an increase of approximately 57 percent since 1996. Video game sales made up $5.8 billion of this total, and computer game sales totaled $1.2 billion. Two major trends in the industry are the growth of mobile and online gaming. Mobile gaming allows users to play games on cell phones, Personal Digital Assistants, and mobile game platforms such as Game Boy. Approximately 43 percent of frequent game players report that they played online games in 2004—an increase of 12 percent since 2002. This popularity is a result of improvements in online functionality of console games such as PlayStation 2 or Xbox and the emergence of multiplayer game options in personal computer–based settings that allow gamers from all over the world to compete against one another. In fact, *Animation World Magazine* reports that there are as many as 420,000 people playing Sony Online Entertainment's *EverQuest,* with more than 100,000 playing at the same time. As a result, game industry professionals who specialize in these areas will have excellent employment opportunities over the next decade. Overall, the computer and video game industry is expected to grow faster than the average over the next decade.

Some of the articles in *Careers in Focus: Computer & Video Game Design* appear in Ferguson's *Encyclopedia of Careers and Vocational Guidance,* but they have been updated and revised with the latest information from the U.S. Department of Labor, professional organizations, and other sources. In addition, articles on the following careers have been written specifically for this book: art directors, artists and animators, producers, sound workers, and video game testers.

The **Quick Facts** section provides a brief summary of the career including recommended school subjects, personal skills, work environment, minimum educational requirements, salary ranges, certification or licensing requirements, and employment outlook. This section also provides acronyms and identification numbers for the following government classification indexes: the *Dictionary of Occupational Titles* (DOT), the *Guide for Occupational Exploration* (GOE), the National Occupational Classification (NOC) index, and the Occupational Information Network (O*NET)-Standard Occupational Classification System (SOC) index. The DOT, GOE, and O*NET-SOC indexes have been created by the U.S. government; the NOC index is Canada's career-classification system. Readers can use the identification numbers listed in the Quick Facts section to access further information about a career. Print editions of the DOT (*Dictionary of Occupational Titles.* Indianapolis, Ind.: JIST Works, 1991) and GOE (*The Complete Guide for Occupational Exploration.* Indianapolis, Ind.: JIST Works, 1993) are available at libraries. Electronic versions of the NOC (http://www23.hrdc-drhc.gc.ca) and O*NET-SOC (http://online.onetcenter.org) are available on the World Wide Web. When no DOT, GOE, NOC, or O*NET-SOC numbers are present, this means that the U.S. Department of Labor or Human Resources Development Canada have not created a numerical designation for this career. In this instance, you will see the acronym "N/A," or not available.

The **Overview** section is a brief introductory description of the duties and responsibilities involved in this career. Often, a career may have a variety of job titles. When this is the case, alternative career titles are presented.

The **History** section describes the history of the particular job as it relates to the overall development of its industry or field.

The **Job** describes the primary and secondary duties of the job.

Requirements discusses high school and postsecondary education and training requirements, any certification or licensing that is necessary, and other personal requirements for success in the job.

Exploring offers suggestions on how to gain experience in or knowledge of the particular job before making a firm educational and financial commitment. The focus is on what can be done while still in high school (or in the early years of college) to gain a better understanding of the job.

The **Employers** section gives an overview of typical places of employment for the job.

Starting Out discusses the best ways to land that first job, be it through the college placement office, newspaper ads, or personal contact.

The **Advancement** section describes what kind of career path to expect from the job and how to get there.

Earnings lists salary ranges and describes the typical fringe benefits.

The **Work Environment** section describes the typical surroundings and conditions of employment—whether indoors or outdoors, noisy or quiet, social or independent. Also discussed are typical hours worked, any seasonal fluctuations, and the stresses and strains of the job.

The **Outlook** section summarizes the job in terms of the general economy and industry projections. For the most part, Outlook information is obtained from the U.S. Bureau of Labor Statistics and is supplemented by information taken from professional associations. Job growth terms follow those used in the *Occupational Outlook Handbook*. Growth described as "much faster than the average" means an increase of 36 percent or more. Growth described as "faster than the average" means an increase of 21 to 35 percent. Growth described as "about as fast as the average" means an increase of 10 to 20 percent. Growth described as "more slowly than the average" means an increase of 3 to 9 percent. Growth described as "little or no change" means an increase of 0 to 2 percent. "Decline" means a decrease of 1 percent or more.

Each article ends with **For More Information,** which lists organizations that provide career information on training, education, internships, scholarships, and job placement.

Careers in Focus: Computer & Video Game Design also includes photos, informative sidebars, and interviews with professionals in the field.

Art Directors

QUICK FACTS

School Subjects
Art
Business
Computer science

Personal Skills
Artistic
Communication/ideas

Work Environment
Primarily indoors
Primarily one location

Minimum Education Level
Bachelor's degree

Salary Range
$48,000 to $68,000 to
$200,000+

Certification or Licensing
None available

Outlook
About as fast as the average

DOT
164

GOE
01.02.03

NOC
5131

O*NET-SOC
27-1011.00

OVERVIEW

Art directors play a key role in every stage of the creation of a video game, from formulating concepts to supervising production. They work with 2D and 3D artists, animators, modelers, and other artistic staff to coordinate all the visual images used in a game. Art directors supervise both in-house and off-site staff, handle management issues, and oversee the entire artistic production process.

HISTORY

The artistic elements of computer and video games have come a long way from *Pong* graphics, where a simple moving blip on the screen entertained early gamers. Today's games not only have to be challenging, engaging, and fun, but they must be visually interesting, realistic, and flashy. While some games still incorporate "cute" characters in the vein of *Q*bert* or *Pac-Man,* the majority of game characters are now human. Figures are pictured with bulging muscles, realistic wounds, or, in the case of many *Final Fantasy* characters, have sex appeal. This realism is the work of huge teams of talented artists that all work together on the completion of a single game. As these teams grew, someone was needed to direct the efforts of these workers and ensure the process, quality, and productivity of the department. Thus, the career of art director developed to oversee this important aspect of game creation.

THE JOB

Art directors are responsible for making sure all visual aspects of a computer or video game meet the expectations of the producers, and ultimately, the client. The art director works directly and indirectly with all artists on a project, such as 2D and 3D artists, model makers, texture artists, and character animators. Depending on the size of the company, the director may work as a staff artist in addition to handling managerial tasks. But generally, the director's main responsibilities focus on board meetings rather than on the drawing board.

Art directors must be skilled in and knowledgeable about design, illustration, computers, research, and writing in order to supervise the work of their department. They need to be skilled in classic art forms, such as illustration and sculpture, while still familiar with computer art tools.

To coordinate all artistic contributions of a computer or video game, art directors may begin with the client's concept or develop one in collaboration with the executive producer. Once the concept is established, the next step is to decide on the most effective way to create it. If the project is to create a sequel to a preexisting game, past animations and illustrations must be taken into consideration and reevaluated for use in the new game.

After deciding what needs to be created, art directors must hire talented staff that can pull it off. Because the visual aspects of a game are so important, the art department can be quite large, even just for the making of a single game.

The process of creating a computer or video game begins in much the same way that a television show or film is created. The art director may start with the client's concept or create one in-house in collaboration with staff members. Once a concept has been created, the art director sketches a rough storyboard based on the producer's ideas, and the plan is presented for review to the creative director. The next step is to develop a finished storyboard, with larger and more detailed frames (the individual scenes) in color. This storyboard is presented to the client for review and used as a guide for the executive producer.

Technology has been playing an increasingly important role in the art director's job. Most art directors, for example, use a variety of computer software programs, including Adobe InDesign, PageMaker, FrameMaker, Illustrator, and Photoshop; as well as more specialized 3D game creation tools such as Lightwave, 3D Studio Max, and Maya.

Art directors may work on more than one game at a time and must be able to keep numerous, unrelated details straight. They often work under pressure of a deadline and yet must remain calm and pleasant when dealing with clients and staff. Because they are supervisors, art

Industry Stats

- Entertainment software sales were $7 billion in 2003—an increase of nearly 57 percent since 1996.

- The computer and video game industry has released more than 7,000 titles since 1994.

- Thirty-five percent of Americans consider game play to be their most fun activity.

- The industry has a bright future, at least according to current game players. More than 50 percent of game players today say they will be playing as much or more in 10 years.

Source: Entertainment Software Association

directors are often called upon to resolve problems, not only with projects but with employees as well.

REQUIREMENTS

High School

A college degree is usually a requirement for art directors; however, in some instances, it is not absolutely necessary. A variety of high school courses will give you both a taste of college-level offerings and an idea of the skills necessary for art directors on the job. These courses include art, drawing, art history, graphic design, illustration, and computer science.

Math courses are also important. Most of the elements of sizing an image involve calculating percentage reduction or enlargement of the original picture. This must be done with a great degree of accuracy if the overall design is going to work. For example, type size may have to be figured within a thirty-second of an inch for a print project. Errors can be extremely costly and may make a game look sloppy.

Other useful courses that you should take in high school include business, technical drawing, and social science.

Postsecondary Training

According to the American Institute of Graphic Arts, nine out of 10 artists have a college degree. Among them, six out of 10 have majored in graphic design, and two out of 10 have majored in fine arts. In addition, almost two out of 10 have a master's degree. Along with general two- and four-year colleges and universities, a number of professional art schools offer two-, three-, or four-year programs with such classes as figure drawing, painting, graphic design, and other art courses, as well as classes in art history, writing, and business administration.

Specialized courses, sometimes offered only at professional art schools, may be particularly helpful for students who want to go into the video and computer game industry. These include animation, Web design, and portfolio development.

Because of the nature of their work, it is essential for art directors to have a thorough understanding of how computer animation and layout programs work. In smaller companies, the art director may be responsible for doing some of this work; in larger companies, staff artists, under the direction of the art director, may use these programs. In either case, the director must be familiar with imaging software and how to use it to best create the intended visual effect.

In addition to course work at the college level, many universities and professional art schools offer graduates or students in their final year a variety of workshop projects or internships. These opportunities provide students with the chance to work on real games, develop their personal styles, and add to their work experience.

Other Requirements

The work of an art director requires creativity, imagination, curiosity, and a sense of adventure. Art directors must be able to work with all sorts of specialized equipment and computer software as well as communicate their ideas to other directors, producers, and clients.

The ability to work well with different people and situations is a must for art directors. They must always be up to date on new techniques, trends, and attitudes. Because deadlines are a constant part of the work, an ability to handle stress and pressure well is key.

The visual aspects of a computer or video game can be the very things that make it sell. For this reason, accuracy and attention to detail are important parts of the art director's job. When the visuals are innovative and clean, the public either clamors for it or pays no notice. But when a project's visuals are done poorly or sloppily, people will notice, even if they have had no artistic training, and the game will not sell.

Other requirements for art directors include time-management skills and an interest in media and people's motivations and lifestyles.

EXPLORING

High school students can get an idea of what an art director does by working on the staff of the school newspaper, magazine, or yearbook. Developing your own artistic talent is important, and this can be accomplished through self-training (reading books about computer and animated art and then applying it on your own) or through formal training in painting, drawing, animation, and other creative arts. At the very least, you should develop your "creative eye," that is, your ability to develop ideas visually. Any art classes will help to develop these skills.

Another way to explore is by researching the career on the Internet. Visit the website of the International Game Developers Association (http://www.igda.org) to check out *Breaking In: Preparing for Your Career in Games*. This free online publication can give you an overview of the different jobs available in the visual arts and features job profiles and interviews of workers in the field.

EMPLOYERS

Art directors working in computer and video game design work all over the country for game companies large and small. The largest employers are located in California, New York, Washington, Maryland, and Illinois. Electronic Arts is the largest independent publisher of interactive entertainment, including several development studios. Big media companies such as Disney have also opened interactive entertainment departments. Jobs should be available at these companies as well as with online services and interactive networks, which are growing rapidly.

STARTING OUT

Since an art director's job requires a great deal of experience, it is usually not considered an entry-level position. Typically, a person on a career track toward art director is hired as an assistant to an established director. Recent graduates wishing to enter the game industry should develop what is called a demo reel. This is a type of portfolio, only the work is interactive and shows moving animations and backgrounds as opposed to pictures of static images. Demo reels can show your skill in composition, color, light, motion, presentation, and craftsmanship. It should reflect a wide breadth of styles and show work in more than just one genre of game. This will show that you are versatile as well as creative.

Remember that art directors have done their time in lower positions before advancing to the level of director, so be willing to do your time and acquire credentials by working on various projects. Starting out as an intern or assistant in an art department is a good way to get experience and develop skills.

ADVANCEMENT

Again, art directors are not entry-level workers. They usually have years of experience working at lower-level jobs in the field before gaining the knowledge needed to supervise projects. This experience will help them manage their artistic staff and solve problems quickly when necessary.

While some may be content upon reaching the position of art director, many art directors take on even more responsibility within their organizations, become game producers, develop original multimedia programs, or create their own games.

Many people who get to the position of art director do not advance beyond the title but move on to work at more prestigious game developers. Competition for positions at companies that have strong reputations continues to be keen because of the sheer number of talented people interested in the field. At smaller game developers, the competition may be less intense, since candidates are competing primarily against others in the local market.

EARNINGS

According to the American Institute of Graphic Arts' *Aquent Salary Survey 2003,* the median salary for art directors was $60,000. Art directors in the 25th percentile earned $48,000 annually, while those in the 75th percentile made $75,000 per year.

The International Game Developers Association (IGDA) reports that artists with one to two years of experience earn approximately $57,000, while art directors with six or more years of experience can earn $68,000 or more. Skilled directors with many years of experience working with some of the larger game developers can earn salaries of $200,000 or more.

Most companies employing art directors offer insurance benefits, a retirement plan, and other incentives and bonuses.

WORK ENVIRONMENT

Art directors usually work in studios or office buildings. While their work areas are ordinarily comfortable, well lit, and ventilated, they often handle glue, paint, ink, and other materials that pose safety hazards, and they should, therefore, exercise caution.

Art directors working in design studios usually work a standard 40-hour week. Many, however, work overtime during busy periods in order to meet deadlines.

While art directors work independently while reviewing artwork, much of their time is spent collaborating with and supervising a team of employees, often consisting of writers, editors, graphic artists, and executives.

OUTLOOK

Computer and video game developers will always need talented artists to produce their programs. People who can quickly and creatively generate new concepts and ideas will be in high demand. IGDA reports that as art and design teams grow larger, the need for skilled art directors will grow as well. Game visuals have become more technical in nature, blurring the line between programmer and artist. Art directors, too, need to become more technical and be able to stay on top of emerging technologies that allow for cutting-edge visual effects.

FOR MORE INFORMATION

For industry information, contact
Entertainment Software Association
1211 Connecticut Avenue, NW, #600
Washington, DC 20036
Email: esa@theesa.com
http://www.theesa.com

For a list of schools specializing in computer art and design and to view student art collections, check out the Education page on the following site:
Gamasutra
600 Harrison Street
3rd Floor
San Francisco, CA 94107
Tel: 415-947-6206
http://www.gamasutra.com/education

For career advice and industry information, contact
International Game Developers Association
600 Harrison Street, 6th Floor
San Francisco, CA 94107
Tel: 415-947-6235
Email: info@igda.org
http://www.igda.org

For information on careers and education, student memberships, and the student newsletter looking.forward, *contact*
IEEE Computer Society
1730 Massachusetts Avenue, NW
Washington, DC 20036-1992
Tel: 202-371-0101
Email: membership@computer.org
http://www.computer.org

INTERVIEW

Raymond Yan is currently the vice president of operations at DigiPen Institute of Technology, in Redmond, Washington. DigiPen is an industry leader in preparing students for careers in the computer and video game industry. Before taking his current position, Mr. Yan was the head of the art department at Nintendo Software Technology for approximately five to six years and was involved with Nintendo titles for the Color Game Boy, N64, GameCube, and Advanced Gameboy. He spoke with the editors of Careers in Focus: Computer & Video Game Design *about his career.*

Q. What were your main duties at Nintendo Software Technology?

A. I was responsible for the art department and handled things such as hiring, assigning artists to projects, and defining the art production pipeline for various game platforms/projects. I also was directly involved with the various projects as both art director and worked as the art production director for a GameCube launch title.

Q. How did you train to do this job?

A. There isn't a specific program that I am aware of that one can take to become an art director. That said, strong art skills, excellent problem solving skills, and strong production management skills are necessary. While many of these skills can be initially developed through a number of good fine arts programs, much of it must be learned simply through a great deal of production experience. Of course, knowledge of current art production tools is good to develop as well.

Like many in the business, I did not get "formalized" training and learned much of what I know on the job. Before game development, I completed an associate degree in broadcasting and worked in this field for a number of years before discovering that 3D animation production was the up and coming thing (this is back in 1991). I ended up joining DigiPen as a 3D animation student and was hired, primarily due to my broadcast production background. As the relationship between DigiPen and Nintendo grew, I was asked to head up the art team for some of the research work Nintendo asked DigiPen to do. In 1997, Nintendo Software Technology was created and I joined to head the art department.

Q. Since the career of art director is not an entry-level position, how does someone get a job in this field?

A. Today's art directors typically have a great deal of production experience (about eight to 10 years) and, within the game industry, you will typically find that art directors have worked their way up the ranks first as production artists, then art lead positions and finally, get the chance to lead an entire art team.

Q. What type of advancement opportunities are available for art directors?

A. Most art directors I know truly enjoy their position and, given that many of them are responsible for the entire art department at a given company, they have already reached the highest position they can as artists. That said, it is possible for art directors to move into more senior management positions within a company.

Q. What is the future employment outlook for art directors?

A. In brief, with the increased demand in quality and quantity of work from artists, the need for good art directors who can ensure that the art team "delivers the goods" has also increased. As a result, these art directors will continue to see many opportunities.

Artists and Animators

OVERVIEW

Game *artists* and *animators* use their computer skills as well as their artistic abilities to produce games that may entertain, test, and even teach players. Artists and animators work as part of a team that develops a concept for a game, the game rules, the various levels of play, and the game story from beginning to end. Depending on the size of the company they work for and the project they are working on, artists and animators may be responsible for working on one specific game aspect, such as *texture* (that is, creating the textured look for each object in the game), or be responsible for working on several game aspects, such as character building, environment, and motion.

HISTORY

The computer video gaming industry is a relatively new field that can trace its roots back to the second half of the 20th century. At that time, computers were still very large machines that were expensive to run and available only in such places as universities and government research laboratories. While a number of people created forerunners to computer video games, the first such game was not developed until several students at the Massachusetts Institute of Technology began working on the idea. In 1962 their efforts resulted in *Spacewar*, the first fully interactive game specifically made to be played on a computer. Steve Russell was the main programmer of *Spacewar* and is considered one of the founders of this field. In 1966, Ralph Baer, an engineer and inventor, created his own video game and game console based on a television set. He continued to work on his invention, which became commercially available as *The Odyssey* in 1972. In addition to Russell and Baer, inventor Nolan Bushnell was instrumental in creating the computer video game industry. While Baer was working on game equipment to be used in the home, Bushnell focused his efforts on arcades, where he thought video games could become commercially successful. His game *Computer Space* was the first video game designed to be played in an arcade. However, the game proved too complicated to operate and it did not become popular. Nevertheless, Bushnell continued his game work, and in 1972 he and programmer Al Alcorn created *Pong*. *Pong* was a simple video game of tennis that became wildly popular and revolutionized the industry.

Once people had caught on to the easy yet addictingly fun game of *Pong*, they were willing to try out other video games and wanted more variety. As game creators worked on developing new games, they improved existing technologies and invented new ones to enhance their work. The development and popularization of equipment, such as home game consoles, personal computers, the Internet, and mobile phones, also meant games could be played in a wide variety of places and at just about any time. And as computer technologies grew ever more sophisticated, the artistic quality of games also improved. Colors, textures, smooth movement, sounds, and multiple levels of play are just some of the game features that have improved over the years and will continue to do so. As games have become more complex and the industry grown, workers have begun to specialize in areas that interest them, such as programming, testing, and artistic quality. Today's game artists and animators are skilled professionals responsible for the look of everything a game player sees on the screen.

THE JOB

Game artists and animators work on the creation of games, which can fall into several categories, including sports, action/adventure, simulation, and education. Today, games are also played in a variety of environments, such as on personal computers, in arcades, over the Internet, and on consoles at home. Additionally, games are typically created to appeal to a certain audience, for example, boys, girls, teens, men in their 20s, or everyone. As they do their work, artists and animators must always keep these factors in mind to ensure that the look they produce will meet the game's requirements.

Artists and animators may work at small, start-up companies that are trying to produce their first big-hit game, or they may work at established companies, producing new games for an already successful series. Because of factors such as company size, personal skills and experience, type of game worked on, and developing technologies, not all game artists and animators have the same responsibilities—or even the same job titles—throughout the industry. Some may specialize on a particular aspect of the game, such as creating the game's environments (for example, a forest, a city, the surface of another planet), while others may work on multiple aspects of a game, such as building a character, animating it, and creating other objects in the game. No matter what their job title or the type of game they work on, however, artists and animators must be able to work as part of a team because several groups, or teams, of people usually work together to produce a game. In addition to the artists and animators, these include people who come up with the game idea and its rules, computer programmers who create the software for the game, and game testers who make sure the game works properly.

Game designers begin the process of developing a video game by considering the intended audience, the type of equipment on which the game will be played, and the number of players to be involved. They collaborate to come up with a workable game idea, game rules, and levels of play. *Conceptual artists* sometimes create storyboards, which sketch out elements of the game, such as characters and action, and set a visual tone that the final product should have. This sketch work does not typically become part of the finished product's "in-game" art. It does, though, give the other artists a visual direction on which to base their work.

Video games are made to look two-dimensional (2D), three-dimensional (3D), or combine both 2D and 3D features. Artists who create in-game art with a 2D look do this by drawing on paper then scanning the work into a computer. Artists who create in-game art that has a 3D look use special computer software to make the artwork inside a computer. Some artists may also build models or sculptures of objects then use a 3D scanner to scan the model into the computer. The artist may then use software to touch-up the image until it has the desired look.

Character artists, also called *character builders,* are responsible for creating the characters in a game. They may draw a variety of sketches to plan out the character whether it is 2D or 3D. Then, to create a 3D character, character artists work on a computer and begin building the character from the inside out. To do this, they use software that generates basic shapes, which they manipulate to create a "skeleton" for the character. The artists then add skin, fur, scales or other types of covering to the skeleton as well as colors and details, such as the eyes.

Background artists, sometimes known as *environmental modelers* or *modelers,* create the game's settings. For example, they may need to create realistic city scenes with various buildings, parking ramps, and streets for different levels of play in the game. They may also need to build backgrounds for imaginary places, such as a planet in another galaxy. Background artists are responsible for providing the right setting for the game, and they must make sure their artwork is in correct proportion to other game elements. To do this for 3D environments, they sketch out their designs on paper, consult with other artists, and use the computer to build the backgrounds. In some cases, the background artist will create objects that are part of the scene, such as the furniture in a room, or items a character might use, like a sword or magic stone. In other cases, another artist—a 3D *object specialist* or *object builder*—will create such items. Once again, this artist must make sure his or her work is in proportion to the other artwork and matches the game's visual style.

Texture artists add detail to all the game's artwork so that the surface of each element appears as it should. Texture artists, for example, make a brick wall in a background look rough and brick-like, make a character in the rain look wet, or make a treasure of jewels sparkle and shine. They work fairly closely with the background artists to ensure that the textures they create match what those artists had envisioned. To build textures, texture artists may draw, paint, or photograph surfaces then scan the images into the computer. They use software to manipulate the texture image and "wrap" it around the object on which they are working.

Animators are responsible for giving movement to the game's characters. They must have an understanding of human anatomy and often model game characters' movements on actual human or animal movement. After all, even if the character is a green, three-eyed alien with wings, it still needs to move smoothly and believably through a scene. In one method of animation, the artist builds a model or sculpture of a character, scans it into the computer, and then uses software to animate the character in the computer. In another method, which is typically used with sports games to create the realistic movements of athletes, actual people are used as models. In this method, called "motion capture," a person wearing body sensors goes through whatever motions the game character will be doing—jumping, throwing a football, running, dribbling a basketball, and so on. The motion sensors send information to a computer and the computer creates a

Two artists study their most recent sketches for a video game. *(Jim Whitmer Photography)*

"skeleton" of the person in motion. The animator then builds on this skeleton, adding skin, clothing, and other details.

Animators are also responsible for getting characters' personalities to show through. They must use their artistic skills to convey feelings, such as anger, fear, and happiness, through a character's facial expressions and body language. Animators may work closely with the character artists and the game designers to get an understanding of each character's personality and goals. That way animators can determine, for example, if a character's smile should be wide and friendly, small and meek, or more like a sneer than a real smile.

All artists and animators must keep practical information in mind as they do their work. The type of equipment a game is designed for, for example, will impose limitations on such elements as the speed of play and the details that will be visible. Artists and animators must also be able to work on schedule, meeting the deadlines set for their stage in the game development process. If an artist comes up with great work but is always missing deadlines, he or she will be delaying the production of the game and perhaps putting the project in jeopardy. Few team members will want to work with someone like that. Additionally, artists and animators need to know how to use available technologies and techniques. Because this work is part of the dynamic computer industry, new equipment and processes are always being developed and refined. Artists and animators must want to keep learning throughout their careers so that their skills are up to date.

REQUIREMENTS

High School

If you are interested in working in the video game field as an artist or animator, you should take art and computer classes in high school. Math classes, such as algebra and geometry, will also be helpful. If your school offers graphic design classes, be sure to take those. Biology classes can offer the opportunity to learn about anatomy and physics can teach you about motion. Most artists and animators today have college degrees, so take classes that will help you prepare for a college education, including history, government, and English.

Postsecondary Training

Many people in this field have degrees in fine arts, graphic arts, or industrial design, but it is possible to enter the field with a degree in another area, such as architecture or computer science. It is important to get a broad-based background in the arts, and traditional arts should not be overlooked. Classes in drawing, sculpture, painting, and color theory will teach you many of the basics artists need to know. Some schools offer classes in animation, and even if you don't plan on becoming an animator, these classes will be helpful to you later in your career. Naturally, computer classes are important to take, and you should try to learn about game art software, such as 3D Studio Max, as well as other software, like Photoshop. And even though artists and animators usually don't do game programming, take computer programming classes to at least learn the basics. The more you understand about all aspects of game development, the better able you'll be to make your artistic contributions enhance a game.

Other Requirements

Game artists and animators must be creative and able to translate their imaginative ideas into visual representations. They should have a keen sense of color, be able to visualize things in three dimensions, and work as part of a group. Like all artists, they are able to give and receive criticism in a fair and impersonal manner. Curiosity and a willingness to learn are important traits that drive artists and animators to use new technologies or try different techniques to get just the right visual effect for something like a character's shadow. Artists and animators should also like to play games themselves. The enjoyment they get from playing, and an understanding of why they like to play games, helps them to be better game makers.

EXPLORING

If you are interested in becoming a game artist or an animator, you can start quite simply by drawing characters and landscapes. You can try copying images from games that you know or create your own characters and settings. Remember, you don't have to be high-tech right away. It's also important to familiarize yourself with the industry, so read publications such as *Game Developer* (http://www. gdmag.com) and *Animation World* (http://mag.awn.com). You also might want to read the online publication *Breaking In: Preparing for Your Career in Games,* which is available at the International Game Developers Association's website, http://www.igda.org/ breakingin. The publication offers an overview of visual arts careers, profiles of workers in the field, and other resources. The association also offers student membership. If you have friends who are interested in gaming, try creating your own game or add to a game that exists already. Local museums often offer summer art classes, and community colleges often have computer courses— check these out.

One thing many industry experts recommend is to attend conferences such as SIGGRAPH and the Game Developers Conference, both of which are annual events. There you will be able to meet people in the business and other enthusiasts, see new games and technologies, and even attend workshops of interest to you. This is a terrific opportunity for networking and, if you are in college, you may hear of internship or job opportunities. Of course, this event can be expensive, but if your funds are limited, you may want to work as a student volunteer and pay much less. Information on the conference and volunteer opportunities is available at http://www.gdconf.com. Information on the SIGGRAPH conference is available at http://www. siggraph.org.

EMPLOYERS

Game artists and animators can work at small companies or start-ups whose focus is the development of only one or two games. They can also work at large companies that are involved in the development of many games at once. In addition, some artists freelance, working with a company for a limited time or on a particular project then moving on to another freelance job with a different company.

Most Popular Game Genres

Video Games
1. Action
2. Sports
3. Racing
4. Role-Playing
5. First-Person
   Shooters
6. Fighting
7. Family Entertainment

Computer Games
1. Strategy
2. Shooter
3. Children's
4. Family Entertainment
5. Role-Playing
6. Sports
7. Adventure
8. Racing
9. Simulation

Source: The NPD Group/NPD Funworld/TRSTS

STARTING OUT

Artists and animators, whether they are just starting out in the field or experienced professionals applying for a job with a new employer, need to have demo reels that highlight their best work. Potential employers will look at a demo reel to get an idea of the artist's or animator's abilities. Those who are seeking their first job can make a reel using artwork that they have done for school as well as anything they've made on their own. Internships also offer an excellent opportunity to gain hands-on experience, which employers like any new hire to have.

To learn of job openings, college students should network with the teachers in their school program, many of whom have contacts in the industry. Conferences, such as SIGGRAPH and the Game Developers Conference, provide major networking opportunities where students can impress those in the field as well as learn of job openings. The Internet is also a good source to use, and websites such as http://www.gamejobs.com and http://www.gamasutra.com offer information on jobs and employers.

ADVANCEMENT

Artists and animators can advance into positions such as *lead artist* and *lead animator.* Their responsibilities can include overseeing the work of a team on a project, going over the artwork of individual members, and keeping the team on their time line. *Art directors* and *animation directors* have even more management responsibilities. They may oversee the work of several teams, assign game projects to teams, plan the time line for a game's development, keep an eye on the budget, and do other administrative tasks. Not all artists and animators want to move into such a position because directors' responsibilities remove them from the hands-on creative process. These artists and animators may choose to advance by continuously upgrading their skills and working in areas of art that they haven't previously tried. With their hard work and broad experience, they can gain a reputation in the industry for the quality and variety of their artwork and become sought-after artists.

EARNINGS

The U.S. Department of Labor does not have specific information on the earnings of video game artists and animators. It does, however, provide wage information for multimedia artists and animators, a group that includes those working on computer games. The median annual salary reported for all multimedia artists and animators was $45,920 in 2003. The lowest paid 10 percent of this group earned $26,830 or less, while the highest paid 10 percent earned $87,090 or more during the same time period. According to the *2003 Game Development Salary Survey* by *Game Developer* magazine, artists with two to five years of experience earned an average of approximately $53,210 and animators with the same amount of experience averaged approximately $56,640 annually.

Artists and animators working for small companies and start-ups may have few if any benefits, such as health insurance and retirement plans. Freelance workers must buy their own health insurance and provide for their retirement themselves. Also, they are not paid during any time off they take for vacations or illnesses. Artists and animators who work for large companies, however, typically receive benefits that include retirement plans, health insurance, and paid vacation and sick days.

WORK ENVIRONMENT

Game artists and animators work primarily indoors and at one location. They work with pens, pencils, and paper as well as with scanners, computers, and other high-tech equipment. The environment is usually casual—business suits are not required—but busy and often fast paced. Although artists and animators typically are required to work a 40-hour workweek, there are often times when they will put in much longer hours as they work to fix any problems with a game and complete it on schedule. Because this is a creative environment, artistic disagreements come up from time to time and egos can be involved. These artists and animators, though, also get great satisfaction from their work and appreciate the opportunity to be in an environment where their creativity is valued.

Many of the jobs in this field are located on the East Coast and West Coast, and those just starting out may need to relocate to get employment. In addition, artists and animators frequently move within the industry, from one employer to another. This helps them gain experience as well as work on a variety of projects and advance their careers.

OUTLOOK

The U.S. Department of Labor estimates that employment for all artists, including multimedia artists and animators, will grow about as fast as the average through 2012. Those within the industry see a bright future as the demand for games continues to grow steadily and technologies make new kinds of games possible. Competition for jobs should be strong since many creative and technically savvy people want to be part of this business.

FOR MORE INFORMATION

For information on animation, contact
Animation World Network
6525 Sunset Boulevard, Garden Suite 10
Hollywood, CA 90028
Tel: 323-606-4200
Email: info@awn.com
http://awn.com

For industry information, contact
Entertainment Software Association
1211 Connecticut Avenue, NW, #600
Washington, DC 20036
Email: esa@theesa.com
http://www.theesa.com

For information on the Game Developers Conference, contact
Game Developers Conference
CMP Media LLC
600 Harrison Street, 3rd Floor
San Francisco, CA 94107
Tel: 415-947-6000
http://www.gdconf.com

For information on careers and to participate in a bulletin board, contact
International Game Developers Association
600 Harrison Street, 6th Floor
San Francisco, CA 94107
Tel: 415-947-6235
Email: info@igda.org
http://www.igda.org

For information on the industry, jobs, and new developments, take a look at this magazine. The website also offers subscription information.
Game Developer
CMP Media LLC
600 Harrison Street, 3rd Floor
San Francisco, CA 94107
http://www.gdmag.com

To read articles from Animation World, visit
Animation World
http://mag.awn.com

Visit these websites for a variety of information and articles on game design, animation, the industry, and more.
GameDev.net
http://www.gamedev.net

GIGnews.com
http://www.gignews.com

Computer and Video Game Designers

OVERVIEW

In the sector of the multibillion-dollar computer industry known as interactive entertainment and recreational computing, *computer and video game designers* create and document the ideas and interactivity for games played on various platforms, or media, such as video consoles and computers, and through online Internet subscriptions. They generate ideas for new game concepts, including sound effects, characters, story lines, and graphics.

Because the industry is fairly new, it is difficult to estimate how many people work as game designers. Approximately 219,000 people work in the computer and video game industry as a whole. Designers either work for companies that make the games or create the games on their own and sell their ideas and programs to companies that produce them.

HISTORY

Computer and video game designers are a relatively new breed. The industry didn't begin to develop until the 1960s and 1970s, when computer programmers at some large universities, big companies, and government labs began designing games on mainframe computers. Steve Russell was perhaps the first video game designer. In 1962, when he was in college, he made up a simple game called *Spacewar*. Graphics of space ships flew through a starry sky on the video screen, the object of the game being to shoot down enemy ships. Nolan Bushnell, another early designer, played *Spacewar* in college. In 1972 he put the first video game in an arcade;

it was a game very much like *Spacewar,* and he called it *Computer Space.* However, many users found the game difficult to play, so it wasn't a success.

Bruce Artwick published the first of many versions of Flight Simulator, and Bushnell later created *Pong,* a game that required the players to paddle electronic ping-pong balls back and forth across the video screen. *Pong* was a big hit, and players spent thousands of quarters in arcade machines all over the country playing it. Bushnell's company, Atari, had to hire more and more designers every week, including Steve Jobs, Alan Kay, and Chris Crawford. These early designers made games with text-based descriptions (that is, no graphics) of scenes and actions with interactivity done through a computer keyboard. Games called *Adventure, Star Trek,* and *Flight Simulator* were among the first that designers created. They used simple commands like "look at building" and "move west." Most games were designed for video machines; not until the later 1970s did specially equipped TVs and early personal computers (PCs) begin appearing.

In the late 1970s and early 1980s, designers working for Atari and Intellivision made games for home video systems, PCs, and video arcades. Many of these new games had graphics, sound, text, and animation. Designers of games like *Pac-Man, Donkey Kong,* and *Space Invaders* were successful and popular. They also started to make role-playing games like the famous *Dungeons and Dragons.* Richard Garriott created *Ultima,* another major role-playing game. Games began to feature the names and photos of their programmers on the packaging, giving credit to individual designers.

Workers at Electronic Arts began to focus on making games for PCs to take advantage of technology that included the computer keyboard, more memory, and floppy disks. They created games like *Carmen Sandiego* and *M.U.L.E.* In the mid- to late 1980s, new technology included more compact floppies, sound cards, and larger memory. Designers also had to create games that would work on more than just one platform—PCs, Apple computers, and 64-bit video game machines.

In the 1990s, Electronic Arts started to hire teams of designers instead of "lone wolf" individuals (those who design games from start to finish independently). Larger teams were needed because games became more complex; design teams would include not only programmers but also artists, musicians, writers, and animators. Designers made such breakthroughs as using more entertaining graphics, creating more depth in role-playing games, using virtual reality in sports games, and using more visual realism in racing games and flight simulators. This new breed of designers created games using techniques like Assembly, C, and HyperCard. By 1994, designers began to use CD-ROM technology to its fullest. In only a few months, *Doom* was a hit. Designers of this game gave players the chance to alter it themselves at various levels, including choices of weapons and enemies. *Doom* still has fans worldwide.

The success of shareware (software that is given away to attract users to want to buy more complete software) has influenced the return of smaller groups of designers. Even the lone wolf is coming back, using shareware and better authoring tools such as sound libraries and complex multimedia development environments. Some designers are finding that they work best on their own or in small teams.

What's on the horizon for game designers? More multiplayer games; virtual reality; improved technology in coprocessors, chips, hardware, and sound fonts; and "persistent worlds," where online games are influenced by and evolve from players' actions. These new types of games require that designers know more and more complex code so that games can "react" to their multiple players.

THE JOB

Designing games involves programming code as well as creating stories, graphics, and sound effects. It is a very creative process, requiring imagination and computer and communication skills to develop games that are interactive and entertaining. As mentioned earlier, some game designers work on their own and try to sell their designs to companies that produce and distribute games; others are employees of companies such as Electronic Arts, Broderbund, and many others. Whether designers work alone or for a company, their aim is to create games that get players involved. Game players want to have fun, be challenged, and sometimes learn something along the way.

Each game must have a story line as well as graphics and sound that will entertain and engage the players. Story lines are situations that the players will find themselves in and make decisions about. Designers develop a plan for combining the story or concept, music or other sound effects, and graphics. They design rules to make it fun, challenging, or educational, and they create characters for the stories or circumstances, worlds in which these characters live, and problems or situations these characters will face.

One of the first steps is to identify the audience that will be playing the game. How old are the players? What kinds of things are they interested in? What kind of game will it be: action, adventure, "edutainment," role-playing, or sports? And which platform will the game use: video (e.g., Nintendo), computer (e.g., Macintosh), or online (Internet via subscription)?

The next steps are to create a design proposal, a preliminary design, and a final game design. The proposal is a brief summary of what the game involves. The preliminary design goes much further, outlining in more detail what the concept is (the story of the game); how the players get involved; what sound effects, graphics, and other elements will be included (What will the screen look like? What kinds of sound effects should the player hear?); and what productivity tools (such as word processors, database programs, spreadsheet programs, flowcharting programs, and prototyping programs) the designer intends to use to create these elements. Independent designers submit a product idea and design proposal to a publisher along with a cover letter and resume. Employees work as part of a team to create the proposal and design. Teamwork might include brainstorming sessions to come up with ideas, as well as involvement in market research (surveying the players who will be interested in the game).

The final game design details the basic idea, the plot, and every section of the game, including the start-up process, all the scenes (such as innings for baseball games and maps for edutainment games), and all the universal elements (such as rules for scoring, names of characters, and a sound effect that occurs every time something specific happens). The story, characters, worlds, and maps are documented. The game design also includes details of the logic of the game, its algorithms (the step-by-step procedures for solving the problems the players will encounter), and its rules; the methods the player will use to load the game, start it up, score, win, lose, save, stop, and play again; the graphic design, including storyboards and sample art; and the audio design. The designer might also include marketing ideas and proposed follow-up games.

Designers interact with other workers and technologists involved in the game design project, including programmers, audio engineers, artists, and even *asset managers*, who coordinate the collecting, engineering, and distribution of physical assets to the *production team* (the people who will actually produce the physical product).

Designers need to understand games and their various forms, think up new ideas, and experiment with and evaluate new designs. They assemble the separate elements (text, art, sound, video) of a game into a complete, interactive form, following through with careful planning and preparation (such as sketching out scripts, storyboards, and design documents). They write an implementation plan and guidelines (How will designers manage the process? How much will it cost to design the game? How long and thorough will the guidelines be?).

Finally, they amend designs at every stage, solving problems and answering questions.

Computer and video game designers often keep scrapbooks, notes, and journals of interesting ideas and other bits of information. They collect potential game material and even catalog ideas, videos, movies, pictures, stories, character descriptions, music clips, sound effects, animation sequences, and interface techniques. The average time it takes to design a game, including all the elements and stages just described, can be from about six to 18 months.

REQUIREMENTS

High School

If you like to play *Madden NFL, Zelda,* or *The Sims,* you're already familiar with games. You will also need to learn a programming language like C++ or Java, and you'll need a good working knowledge of the hardware platform for which you plan to develop your games (video, computer, online). In high school, learn as much as you can about computers: how they work, what kinds there are, how to program them, and any languages you can learn. You should also take physics, chemistry, and computer science. Since designers are creative, take courses such as art, literature, and music as well.

Postsecondary Training

Although, strictly speaking, you don't have to have a college degree to be a game designer, most companies are looking for creative people who also have a degree. Having one shows that you've been actively involved in intense, creative work; that you can work with others and follow through on assignments; and, of course, that you've learned what there is to know about programming, computer architecture (including input devices, processing devices, memory and storage devices, and output devices), and software engineering. Employers want to know that you've had some practical experience in design.

A growing number of schools offer courses or degrees in game design. The University of North Texas, for example, has a Laboratory for Recreational Computing (LARC) that offers two senior elective courses: game programming and advanced game programming. For more information, visit http://larc.csci.unt.edu. One of the best-known degree-granting schools is DigiPen Institute of Technology (http://www.digipen.edu) in Redmond, Washington, with programs both at the associate and bachelor's level. For a list of schools in the United States, visit http://www.igda.org/breakingin/resource_schools.php. The college courses you should take include programming (including assembly level), computer architecture, software engineering, computer graphics, data structures, algorithms, communication networks, artificial intelligence (AI) and expert systems, interface systems, mathematics, and physics.

According to Professor Ian Parberry of the LARC, the quality of your education depends a lot on you. "You must take control of your education, seek out the best professors, and go beyond the material presented in class. What you have a right to expect from an undergraduate computer science degree is a grasp of the fundamental concepts of computer science and enough practical skills to be able to grow, learn, and thrive in any computational environment, be it computer games or otherwise."

Other Requirements

One major requirement for game design is that you must love to play computer games. You need to continually keep up with technology, which changes fast. Although you might not always use them, you need to have a variety of skills, such as writing stories, programming, and designing sound effects.

You must also have vision and the ability to identify your players and anticipate their every move in your game. You'll also have to be able to communicate well with programmers, writers, artists, musicians, electronics engineers, production workers, and others.

You must have the endurance to see a project through from beginning to end and also be able to recognize when a design should be scrapped.

EXPLORING

One of the best ways to learn about game design is to try to develop copies of easy games, such as *Pong* and *Pac-Man,* or try to change a game that has an editor. (Games such as *Klik & Play, Empire,* and *Doom* allow players to modify them to create new circumstances.)

For high school students interested in finding out more about how video games and animations are produced, the DigiPen Institute of Technology offers a summer workshop. Summertime sessions provide hands-on experience and advice on courses to take in high school to prepare yourself for postsecondary training.

Writing your own stories, puzzles, and games helps develop storytelling and problem-solving skills. Magazines such as *Computer Graphics World* (http://www.cgw.com) and *Game Developer* (http://www.gdmag.com) have articles about digital video and high-end imaging and other technical and design information.

A game designer works on a story line for a game. *(Jim Whitmer Photography)*

EMPLOYERS

Software publishers (such as Electronic Arts and Activision) are found throughout the country, though most are located in California, New York, Washington, Maryland, and Illinois. Electronic Arts is the largest independent publisher of interactive entertainment, including several development studios; the company is known worldwide. Big media companies such as Disney have also opened interactive entertainment departments. Jobs should be available at these companies as well as with online services and interactive networks, which are growing rapidly.

Some companies are involved in producing games only for video; others produce only for computers; others make games for various platforms.

STARTING OUT

There are a couple of ways to begin earning money as a game designer: independently or as an employee of a company. It is more realistic to get any creative job you can in the industry (for example, as an artist, a play tester, a programmer, or a writer) and learn as you go, developing your design skills as you work your way up to the level of designer.

Contact company websites and sites that advertise job openings, such as Game Jobs (http://www.gamejobs.com) and Spherion Jobs (http://www.spherion.com/corporate/careercenter/home.jsp).

In addition to a professional resume, it's a good idea to have your own website, where you can showcase your demos. Make sure you have designed at least one demo or have an impressive portfolio of design ideas and documents.

Other ways to find a job in the industry include going to job fairs (such as the Game Developers Conference), where you find recruiters looking for creative people to work at their companies, and checking in with game developer forums and user groups, which often post jobs on the Internet.

ADVANCEMENT

Just as with many jobs, to have better opportunities to advance their position and possibly earn more money, computer and video game designers have to keep up with technology. They must be willing to constantly learn more about design, the industry, and even financial and legal matters involved in development.

Becoming and remaining great at their job may be a career-long endeavor for computer and video game designers, or just a stepping stone to another area of interactive entertainment. Some designers start out as artists, writers, or programmers, learning enough in these jobs to eventually design. For example, a person entering this career may begin as a 3D animation modeler and work through game life cycles to understand what it takes to be a game designer. He or she may decide to specialize in another area, such as sound effects or even budgeting.

Some designers rise to management positions, such as president or vice president of a software publisher. Others write for magazines and books, teach, or establish their own game companies.

EARNINGS

Most development companies spend up to two years designing a game even before any of the mechanics (such as writing final code and drawing final graphics) begin; more complex games take even longer. Companies budget $1 million to $3 million for developing just one game. If the game is a success, designers are often rewarded with bonuses. In addition to bonuses or royalties (the percentage of profits designers receive from each game that is sold), designers' salaries are affected by their amount of professional experience, their location in the country, and the size of their employer. Gama Network, an organization serving electronic games developers, surveyed subscribers, members, and attendees of its three divisions (*Game Developer* magazine, Gamasutra.com, and Game Developers Conference) to find out what professionals in the game development industry were earning. The survey reveals that game designers with one to two years' experience had an average annual salary of approximately $41,652. Those with three to five years of experience averaged $53,031 annually, and those with more than six years of experience averaged $64,248 per year. Lead designers/creative directors earned higher salaries, ranging from $44,667 for those with less than two years of experience to $92,059 for workers with six or more years of experience in the field. It is important to note that these salaries are averages, and some designers (especially those at the beginning stages of their careers) earn less than these amounts. These figures, however, provide a useful guide for the range of earnings available.

Any major software publisher will likely provide benefits such as medical insurance, paid vacations, and retirement plans. Designers who are self-employed must provide their own benefits.

WORK ENVIRONMENT

Computer and video game designers work in office settings, whether at a large company or a home studio. At some companies, artists and designers sometimes find themselves working 24 or 48 hours at a time, so the office areas are set up with sleeping couches and other areas where employees can relax. Because the game development industry is competitive, many designers find themselves under a lot of pressure from deadlines, design problems, and budget concerns.

OUTLOOK

Computer and video games are a fast-growing segment of the U.S. entertainment industry. In fact, The NPD Group, a market information provider, reports that sales of computer and video games reached $7 billion in 2003. As the demand for new games, more sophisticated games, and games to be played on new systems grows, more and more companies will hire skilled people to create and perfect these products. Opportunities for game designers, therefore, should be good.

In any case, game development is popular; the Interactive Digital Software Association estimates that about 60 percent of the U.S. population (approximately 145 million people) play computer and video games. People in the industry expect more and more integration of interactive entertainment into mainstream society. Online development tools such as engines, graphic and sound libraries, and programming languages such as Java will probably create opportunities for new types of products that can feature game components.

FOR MORE INFORMATION

For information on associate and bachelor of science degrees in computer animation and simulation, contact
DigiPen Institute of Technology
5001-150th Avenue, NE
Redmond, WA 98052
Tel: 425-558-0299
Email: info@digipen.edu
http://www.digipen.edu

For industry information, contact
Entertainment Software Association
1211 Connecticut Avenue, NW, #600
Washington, DC 20036
Email: esa@theesa.com
http://www.theesa.com

For comprehensive career information, including Breaking In: Preparing For Your Career in Games, *visit the IGDA website.*
International Game Developers Association
600 Harrison Street, 6th Floor
San Francisco, CA 94107
Phone: 415-947-6235
Email: info@igda.org
http://www.igda.org

For information on training programs to become game designers and programmers, contact
Laboratory for Recreational Computing
University of North Texas
Department of Computer Science
PO Box 311277
Denton, TX 76203
Tel: 940-565-2681
Email: ian@cs.unt.edu
http://larc.csci.unt.edu

INTERVIEW

Steve Ince is an award-nominated writer-designer in the game industry. He spoke with the editors of Careers in Focus: Computer & Video Game Design *about his career.*

Q. How did you get into this career?

A. I was concentrating on my artistic side at the time and was told that Revolution Software was looking for an artist. My portfolio and enthusiasm, as well as proving myself through a month's trial, got me the job. It was only later that I moved over into a designer and writer role.

Q. What are your main and secondary job duties as a designer?

A. I've only worked with story-driven games, so my duties may not be typical of designers in other genres or styles of game. My primary job duties are to develop the broad outline of the design so that it matches the agreed-upon vision of the game and that it works well with the story. I would then build up the detail so that everything that happens in the game is clearly documented. This includes outlines of dialogue scenes, puzzle designs, location descriptions, character descriptions, and interface mechanics.

The secondary duties are to work with the other departments to ensure that the design is clear and not too demanding on the budget and schedule. Modifications and redesign often follows this.

Q. What makes for a good design?

A. Ensuring that the gameplay offers a challenge at the same time as being fun. There should be a feeling of constant progression and the player should always know what their current objective is. It may be something as simple as getting through the locked door, but as long as the player knows they have to get through that door they can address that objective. The solutions can vary from finding the grenade to blow it open to winning the speeder race so that you can get enough money to buy the security override device. Whatever the solution to an obstacle is, if the solution has an elegance to it that causes no frustration, then you're on a winner.

Q. How long does it take to design a typical game?

A. At least six months, and often much more for a game with a complex plot and intricate character relationships. Detailing up the game sections can take up to a month each, depending on the size of the section. This often involves a team of up to four or five working in parallel and brainstorming each other's sections on a regular basis.

Q. I notice at your website that you have achieved acclaim for your work as a game writer. How closely linked are the careers of designer and writer? Are most designers also writers and vice versa, or are they typically specialized occupations?

A. They can be completely independent of each other or they can overlap to the point where one person can do both completely. Although a writer doesn't have to be a designer, it works better if they at least have an understanding of the design process and the constraints and limitations of the genre in which they are expecting to work. Designers should have a modicum of writing skills because they will have to create documents that need to describe the design in a clear manner. Sometimes a writer may be asked to tidy up documentation, particularly if the documents form part of a pitch proposal.

Although many designers have excellent writing skills when it comes down to design documentation, they may be a little out of their depth when it comes to areas of story, characters, and dialogue—unless, of course, the designer is also skilled in those areas. An experienced writer will automatically know the difference between story and plot. They will know about character motivation, scene construction, escalating conflict, the expectation gap, etc.

Q. What are the keys to a well-written game script?

A. Dynamic scenes of a type you would expect to see in a top film or TV show. Character conflict can be handled with more subtlety in games today and should be done so. It can be easy to fall into the trap of turning exposition into a weary monologue. Avoid this by breaking it up into a number of smaller scenes and put it over in a dynamic way. Make it feel like the player is working to get the information instead of simply triggering it by walking through a door. Ensure that all characters in the game stay in character. Maintain the suspension of disbelief at all times and don't throw anything in that breaks this. Make sure that there are strong story reasons that the character moves from one section to another. Write the dialogue to match the vision and genre of the game. Don't overstate things; play to the intelligence of the player who will fill in blanks if the scenes are handled well.   Avoid stock characters at all times.

Q. What are the most important personal and professional qualities for designers and writers, respectively?

A. On a personal level, both designers and writers have to be prepared for incredibly hard work and to be able to accept major disappointment. Looming deadlines always create pressure to complete a task in less time than would be ideal, but it is something that needs to be addressed with hard work. Then, when you think that everything is complete, it could be decided that the design or story is too large and sections need to be cut. There's nothing worse than the feeling that a month's work has been for nothing, but you have to have the strength to handle it and move on.

On a professional level, you should always deliver. Don't get a reputation for always delivering late or delivering substandard work. Accept compliments and unpleasant decisions with the same good grace. Always look at the bigger picture, the project's vision, in a positive light. Always work towards the good of the project and always portray this in your work with other members of the team.

Q. What is your favorite game that you have worked on and why?

A. *Broken Sword-The Sleeping Dragon* (http://www.brokenswordgame. com), the third in the Broken Sword trilogy. I was involved in the development of the story and design from the ground up, and this led me to be able to develop new ideas in the approach to how we handled both the logic that structured the scenes, and the acting within the scenes. With script functions that allowed the controlling of camera cuts, body language, facial expressions, and the dynamics of the dialogue, even the smallest of scenes could be given a highly cinematic feel. This supported the actual script writing in an incredibly satisfying way.

Computer Programmers

OVERVIEW

Computer programmers work in the field of electronic data processing. They write instructions in a computer language, or code, that the computer understands and that tell computers what to do. Computer programmers who work in the computer and video game industry write code for computer and video games played on various platforms, such as video game consoles, arcade machines, handheld devices, and computers, and through online Internet subscriptions. There are approximately 499,000 computer programmers employed in the United States.

HISTORY

Computers have been used to process large amounts of data in business, government, and education since the 1950s. It was only a matter of time before someone figured out a way to have fun with them. The computer and video game industry began to develop in the 1960s and 1970s, when computer programmers at some large universities, big companies, and government labs began designing games on mainframe computers. *Spacewar*, generally considered to be the first video game, was developed in 1962 by a team led by Steve Russell, who was a student at the Massachusetts Institute of Technology. *Spacewar* quickly spread to other university computer labs and was very popular. Computer and video games stepped out of the university setting and into the public in the early 1970s. In 1972, Nolan Bushnell founded the Atari company and created *Pong*, the first popular video arcade game. *Pong* required players to paddle electronic ping-pong balls back and forth across the video screen. The game was a big hit, and players spent countless quarters in arcade machines all over the country playing it. In the years following, more games were developed.

Most games developed thus far were designed for video arcade machines. It wasn't until the mid- to late-1970s that games for specially equipped TVs and personal computers (PCs) begin appearing. The Atari 2600, Intellivision, and the Commodore 64 were some of the early platforms used to play games at home. Games and their platforms continued to evolve. In the 1980s and 1990s, game players were introduced to new systems and games from Nintendo, Sega, and Sony, as well as from some of the original computer game companies. Games were also developed for PCs at an increasing rate as PC sales increased. In 2001 computer software giant Microsoft got in the game, so to speak, with the introduction of its Xbox platform and games. Computer game programmers were kept busy as they constantly strived to develop new ideas and come up with the next big computer and video game before another company did. All of the competition transformed the computer and video game industry: across all platforms, the rudimentary graphics and action-driven premises of the early games had been replaced with cutting-edge animation, graphics, sound, and game strategy.

Looking to the future, the trend is towards programming for more multiplayer games—online games where players from around the block or world can play against one another on the Internet—as well as programming for more emphasis on artificial intelligence, where computer game characters appear to be intelligent beings who react to players and whose actions are determined by the players' actions.

THE JOB

In the past, one programmer might have worked on a game, handling every task associated with its creation. As games became more complex, this was no longer the case. Because there are now several different specialty areas of programming in the computer and video game industry, no one programmer is responsible for all aspects of a game. The following are typical specialty areas for programming for the computer and video game industry: engine programmers, tools programmers, Artificial Intelligence programmers, audio programmers, and graphics programmers.

Engine programmers create the base, or the engine, of a game. By writing the necessary software for the game to run, they construct the underlying technical base upon which all other aspects of the game are built.

Tools programmers make the tools that others use to develop the game. Most nontechnical workers on a game—artists and designers, for example—are concerned with the art, sound, and storyline aspects of a game, not the computer code required to apply these aspects to the game. But the computer code is integral to the creation of a game. Tools programmers write software that converts design elements of a game into computer code or data that works with the engine of the game. The nontechnical workers on a game can then use these tools to add their creations to a game much faster than if they did not have such tools.

Artificial Intelligence (AI) programmers write the code that causes computer game characters to act in a realistic manner. AI programmers create a set of rules to direct the behavior of the characters as they encounter various scenarios throughout the course of play in a game.

Audio or sound programmers write the software necessary to implement the sound and music in a game.

Graphics or graphics game programmers write the software necessary to implement the graphics in a game. They often collaborate with the artists working on a game.

Other specialty titles found the in field of computer game programming include *networking programmers,* who focus on how to add a multiplayer component to a game; *interface programmers,* who focus on user interface systems (the "user" being the game player); and *QA programmers,* who create tools to test games for quality assurance issues.

Other titles, such as *entry-level programmer, associate programmer, junior programmer, lead programmer,* and *senior programmer,* are titles that correspond with the level of experience, education, and/or supervisory responsibilities of a position, rather than the area of specialty of the position. These titles are explained in greater detail in the "Advancement" section of this article.

Some job aspects of programming in the computer and video game industry are the same, regardless of the area of specialty. A game designer will present their game concept to the programmer and request that the programmer write the necessary code to realize this concept. Before actually writing code for part of a game, the programmer must analyze the designer's request and the desired results. The programmer must decide how to approach it and plan what the computer will have to do to produce the desired results. They must pay attention to minute details and instruct the computer in each step of the process. These instructions are coded in one of several programming languages, such as C/C++, Java, or Assembly. When the program is completed, the programmer tests its working practicality. If the game responds according to expectations, the programmer is finished. If the game does not respond as anticipated, the program will have to be debugged—that is, examined for errors that must be eliminated. Games that are designed to play on a platform other than a personal computer, such as a video game console, arcade machine, or handheld gaming device, are then tested by the hardware manufacturer to ensure the game performs well on the intended platform.

REQUIREMENTS

High School
In high school you should take any computer programming or computer science courses that are available. You should also concentrate on math, science, and schematic drawing courses, since these subjects directly prepare students for careers in computer programming.

Postsecondary Training
Most employers prefer their programmers to be college graduates. In the past, as the field was first taking shape, employers were known to hire people with some formal education and little or no experience but determination and the ability to learn quickly. As the market becomes saturated with individuals wishing to break into this field, however, a college degree is becoming increasingly important. In fact, as programming for computer and video games becomes more complex, some employers prefer employees with graduate degrees. The U.S. Department of Labor reports that about 65 percent of computer programmers held a bachelor's degree or higher in 2002.

Many personnel officers administer aptitude tests to determine an applicant's potential for programming work. Some employers send new employees to computer schools or in-house training sessions before the employees can assume programming responsibilities. Training periods may last as long as a few weeks, months, or even a year.

Many junior and community colleges also offer two-year associate's degree programs in computer programming and other computer-related technologies.

Most four-year colleges and universities have computer science departments with a variety of computer-related majors, any of which could prepare a student for a career in programming.

As more and more schools tailor programs specifically to the computer and video game industry, you may have the opportunity to earn a degree or certificate in this field.

Employers who require a college degree often do not express a preference as to major field of study, although mathematics or computer science is highly favored. Other acceptable majors may be engineering or physics. Graduate degrees with an emphasis in areas such as Artificial Intelligence or 3D graphics programming are very relevant to the rapidly evolving technology of the computer and video game industry.

Certification or Licensing

Computer programmers might consider becoming certified by the Institute for Certification of Computing Professionals (see the "For More Information" section at the end of this article). Although it is not required, certification may boost an individual's attractiveness to employers during the job search.

Other Requirements

Personal qualifications such as a high degree of reasoning ability, patience, and persistence, as well as an aptitude for mathematics, are important for computer programmers. In the computer and video game industry the work can be stressful, unpredictable, and demanding, so flexibility, enthusiasm, and a love for computer and video games are especially important

Outside of the computer and video game industry, some employers whose work is highly technical require that programmers be qualified in the area in which the firm or agency operates. Engineering firms, for example, prefer young people with an engineering background and are willing to train them in some programming techniques. For other firms, such as banks, consumer-level knowledge of the services that banks offer may be sufficient background for incoming programmers.

EXPLORING

If you are interested in becoming a computer programmer in the computer and video game industry, you might want to read the online publication, *Breaking In: Preparing For Your Career in Games,* which is available at the International Game Developers Association's website, http://www.igda.org/breakingin. The publication offers an overview of programming careers, profiles of workers in the field, and other resources. You might also consider joining the association as a student member.

Another way to learn about this career is to visit a company that produces computer and video games and make an appointment to talk with one of the programmers on the staff.

It is a good idea to start early and get some hands-on experience operating and programming a computer. A trip to the local library or bookstore is likely to turn up books on computer programming in general, as well as computer and video game programming. Joining a computer club and reading professional magazines are other ways to become more familiar with this career field. In addition, you should explore the Internet, a great source of information about computer-related careers and the computer and video game industry. Of course, playing lots of different types of computer and video games is also a great way to become familiar with the various products of the industry.

High school and college students who have experience with computers and computer and video games may be able to obtain part-time jobs or internships in companies that produce computer and video games.

EMPLOYERS

Computer programmers in the computer and video game industry typically work for small, independent game development studios, large computer and video game publishers, or manufacturers of the various computer and video game platforms. These companies are usually located in major cities, especially on the East and West Coasts.

Computer programmers can work in other businesses, such as manufacturing companies, data processing service firms, hardware and software companies, banks, insurance companies, credit companies, publishing houses, government agencies, and colleges and universities throughout the country. Many programmers are employed by businesses as consultants on a temporary or contractual basis. There are approximately 499,000 computer programmers in the United States, and they work in locations across the country and in almost every type of business.

STARTING OUT

You can look for an entry-level programming position in the computer and video game industry in the same way as most other jobs; there is no special or standard point of entry into the field. Individuals with the necessary qualifications should apply directly to companies, or to agencies that have announced job openings through a school placement office, an employment agency, or the classified ads. Any previous experience with writing code for games is worth mentioning on your resume, cover letter, and in interviews. Even if it was for a school project, or something done on your own time for fun, it still counts as experience. It shows what you are capable of doing as well as your potential, demonstrates your motivation, and may help you get your foot in the door at a game company. Students in two- or four-year degree programs should work closely with their schools' placement offices, since major employers often list job openings with such offices.

One thing to keep in mind when looking for employment in the computer and video game industry is geographical location. While there are game companies in most major cities, most are located in cities on the East or West Coasts—San Francisco, Seattle, and New York, for example. You may need to consider relocating to boost your chances of finding a job in the computer and video game industry.

ADVANCEMENT

Programmers are often ranked by such terms as entry-level, associate, junior, or senior programmers. These titles are based on education, experience, and level of responsibility. After programmers have attained the highest available programming rank, they can choose to make other career moves in order to advance further. Some programmers may wish to become a *lead programmer*. These programmers typically are in charge of a group of programmers. In addition to being top-notch programmers, they also need to know how to manage their team of programmers, deal with upper-level management, and interact with other departments that contribute to development of a computer game. These programmers need to have excellent interpersonal skills and enjoy motivating others to perform hard work and strive for excellence. Other management options a programmer might choose to pursue include director, vice president, or other upper-level administrative positions in the computer and video game industry. However, as the level of management responsibilities increases, the amount of technical work performed decreases, so management positions are not for everyone. In general, programming provides a solid background in the computer industry. Experienced programmers enjoy a wide variety of possibilities for career advancement in many computer-related fields.

EARNINGS

According to the National Association of Colleges and Employers, the average starting salary for college graduates with computer programming bachelor's degrees was $45,558 in 2003. The U.S. Department of Labor reports the median annual salary for computer programmers was $60,290 in 2002. The lowest paid 10 percent of programmers earned less than $35,080 annually, and at the other end of the pay scale, the highest paid 10 percent earned more than $96,860 that same year. According to the International Game Developers Association computer programmers employed in the computer and video game industry earned salaries that range from $55,000 (for a programmer with one or two years of experience) to $85,000 (for a lead programmer). The average salary for programmers employed in this industry is $62,500. Top salaries in this industry may reach as high as $300,000.

Most programmers receive the customary paid vacation and sick leave and are included in such company benefits as group insurance and retirement benefit plans.

WORK ENVIRONMENT

Most programmers work in physically pleasant office conditions, since computers require an air-conditioned, dust-free environment. At some companies, programmers sometimes find themselves working more than 24 hours at a time, so the office areas are set up with sleeping couches and other areas where employees can relax. Programmers perform most of their duties in one primary location but may be asked to travel to other computing sites on occasion. Due to long workdays, deadline pressure, and job instability, the computer and video game industry can be a stressful environment in which to work.

Most programmers work more than 40 hours a week. A 2004 International Game Developers Association survey indicated that 38 percent of those polled work 46 to 55 hours a week, and almost 20 percent work more than 55 hours a week on a regular basis. When facing greater than usual deadlines, 35 percent of those polled work 65 to 80 hours a week. The increase in hours worked might be the result of demands for a game to be released by a certain date, for example.

OUTLOOK

Employment for computer programmers is expected to increase about as fast as the average through 2012, according to the U.S. Department of Labor.

Job applicants with the best chances of employment will be college graduates with knowledge of several programming languages, especially newer ones used for computer networking and database management. Competition for jobs will be heavier among graduates of two-year data processing programs and among people with equivalent experience or with less training. Since the computer and video game industry is constantly changing, programmers should stay abreast of the latest technology to remain competitive.

FOR MORE INFORMATION

For more information about careers in computer programming, contact the following organizations:

Association for Computing Machinery
1515 Broadway
New York, NY 10036
Tel: 800-342-6626
Email: sigs@acm.org
http://www.acm.org

Association of Information Technology Professionals
401 North Michigan Avenue
Suite 2200
Chicago, IL 60611-4267
Tel: 800-224-9371
Email: aitp_hq@aitp.org
http://www.aitp.org

For industry information, contact
Entertainment Software Association
1211 Connecticut Avenue, NW, #600
Washington, DC 20036
Email: esa@theesa.com
http://www.theesa.com

Gamasutra
CMP Media LLC
600 Harrison Street
3rd Floor
San Francisco, CA 94107
Tel: 415-947-6206
http://www.gamasutra.com

For career advice and industry information, contact
International Game Developers Association
600 Harrison Street, 6th Floor
San Francisco, CA 94107
Tel: 415-947-6235
Email: info@igda.org
http://www.igda.org

For information on certification programs, contact
Institute for Certification of Computing Professionals
2350 East Devon Avenue, Suite 115
Des Plaines, IL 60018-4610
Tel: 800-843-8227
http://www.iccp.org

Graphics Programmers

OVERVIEW

Graphics programmers design software that allows computers to generate graphic designs, charts, and illustrations for manufacturing, communications, entertainment, and engineering. They also develop computer applications that graphic designers use to create multimedia presentations, posters, logos, layouts for publication, and many other objects. Graphics programmers in the computer and video game industry focus on designing software and writing code in order to create the exciting action and elaborate settings of computer and video games.

HISTORY

Computers have been used to process large amounts of data in business, government, and education since the 1950s. It was only a matter of time before someone figured out a way to have fun with them. The computer and video game industry began to develop in the 1960s and 1970s, when computer programmers at some large universities, big companies, and government labs began designing games on mainframe computers. *Spacewar*, generally considered to be the first video game, was developed in 1962 by a team led by Steve Russell at Massachusetts Institute of Technology. Graphics of space ships flew through a starry sky on the video screen, the object of the game being to shoot down enemy ships. *Spacewar* quickly spread to other university computer labs and was very popular.

Computer and video games stepped out of the university setting and into the public realm in the early 1970s. In 1972, Nolan Bushnell

QUICK FACTS

School Subjects
Art
Computer science

Personal Skills
Artistic
Technical/scientific

Work Environment
Primarily indoors
Primarily one location

Minimum Education Level
Bachelor's degree

Salary Range
$35,080 to $60,290 to $96,860+

Certification or Licensing
Voluntary

Outlook
About as fast as the average

DOT
030

GOE
11.01.01

NOC
2174

O*NET-SOC
15-1021.00

founded the Atari company and created *Pong*, the first popular video arcade game. *Pong* required players to paddle electronic ping-pong balls back and forth across the video screen. The graphics were crude by today's standards, but the game was a big hit all over the country. In the years following, more games were developed, and most were designed for video arcade machines. It wasn't until the mid- to late 1970s that games for specially equipped TVs and personal computers (PCs) begin appearing. The Atari 2600, Intellivision, and the Commodore 64 were some of the early platforms used to play games at home. Games and their platforms continued to evolve, and the graphics improved as computer technology advanced. In the 1980s and 1990s, game players were introduced to new systems and games from Nintendo, Sega, and Sony, as well as from some of the original computer and video game companies. Games were also developed for PCs at an increasing rate as PC sales increased. In 2001 computer software giant Microsoft released its Xbox platform and games. Computer game programmers were kept busy as they constantly strived to develop new ideas and come up with the next big computer and video game before another company did. This competition transformed the computer and video game industry: across all platforms, the rudimentary graphics and simple, action-driven premises of the early games had been replaced with cutting-edge animation, graphics, sound, and game strategy.

In the future, graphics programmers will continue to push the envelope with what can be achieved with their programming, with the goal of perfecting the art of fitting blockbuster graphics and animation within the limitations of what can be displayed in real time on a computer.

THE JOB

Graphics or graphics game programmers write the software necessary to implement the graphics in a computer or video game. The graphics programmer's job is similar to that of other computer programmers: determining what the computer will be expected to do and writing instructions for the computer that will allow it to carry out these functions. For a computer to perform any operation at all, detailed instructions must be written into its memory in a computer language, such as BASIC, COBOL, PASCAL, C++, HTML, Smalltalk, Java, or Assembly. The programmer is responsible for telling the computer exactly what to do. However, graphics are challenging—the programmer needs to project the appearance of three-dimensional objects inside of a two-dimensional display. They also need to

Top Games
(by total U.S. units sold)
VIDEO GAMES

Title	Publisher	Entertainment Software Rating Board (ESRB) Rating
1. Madden NFL 2004	Electronic Arts	Everyone
2. Pokemon Ruby	Nintendo of America	Everyone
3. Pokemon Sapphire	Nintendo of America	Everyone
4. Need for Speed: Underground	Electronic Arts	Everyone
5. Zelda: The Wind Waker	Nintendo of America	Everyone

COMPUTER GAMES

Title	Publisher	ESRB Rating
1. The Sims: Superstar Expansion Pack	Electronic Arts	Teen
2. The Sims Deluxe	Electronic Arts	Teen
3. Command & Conquer: Generals	Electronic Arts	Teen
4. Warcraft III: Frozen Throne Expansion Pack	Blizzard Entertainment	Teen
5. The Sims: Makin' Magic Expansion Pack	Electronic Arts	Teen

Source: The NPD Group/NPD Funworld/TRSTS, 2003

accomplish this goal with writing code that allows for the highest quality of graphics but within the limitations of what can be displayed in real time on a computer.

In order to create graphics for a computer and video game, typically an artist or game designer will present the concept of what they are trying to achieve to the graphics programmer and expect that they will write the necessary code to accomplish the goal. Before actually writing code for part of a game, the programmer must analyze the artist/designer's request and the desired results. The graphics programmer must decide on how to approach it and plan what the computer will have to do to produce the desired results. They must pay attention to minute details and instruct the computer in each step of the process. These instructions are coded in one of several programming languages or implemented through the use of an Application Programming Interface (API), such as Direct 3D. When the graphics code is completed, the programmer tests its working practicality. If the graphics perform according to expectations and the artists and/or designers are satisfied with the end result, it is finished. If the graphics do not perform as anticipated, the graphics code will have to be debugged—that is, examined for errors that must be eliminated. Games that are designed to play on a platform other than a personal computer, such as a video game console, arcade machine, or handheld gaming device, are then tested by the hardware manufacturer to ensure that all aspects of the game, including the graphics, perform well on the intended platform.

REQUIREMENTS

High School

If you are interested in graphics programming in the computer and video game industry, take classes that satisfy the admission requirements of the college or university that you plan to attend. Most major universities have requirements for English, mathematics, science, and foreign languages. Other classes that are useful include physics, statistics, logic, computer science, and, if available, drafting. Since graphics programmers have to have an artistic sense of layout and design, art and photography courses can also be helpful.

Postsecondary Training

A bachelor's degree in computer science or a related field is highly recommended for anyone wishing to enter the field of graphics programming. In fact, as programming for computer and video games becomes more complex, some employers prefer employees with graduate degrees. The U.S. Department of Labor reports that about 65 percent of computer programmers held a bachelor's degree or higher in 2002. It is not a good idea, however, to major in graphics programming exclusively, unless you plan to go on to earn a master's degree or doctorate in the field. According to the Special Interest Group on Computer Graphics, a division of the Association for Computing Machinery (ACM SIGGRAPH), it is better for you to concentrate on the area in which you plan to use computer graphics skills, such as art or engineering, rather than focusing on graphics classes.

Because there are many specialties within the field of computer graphics, such as art, mapmaking, animation, and computer-aided design, you should examine the courses of study offered in several schools before choosing the one you wish to attend. As more and more schools tailor programs specifically to the computer and video game industry, you may have the opportunity to earn a degree or certificate in this field. Graduate degrees with an emphasis in areas such as 3D graphics programming are very relevant to the rapidly evolving technology of the computer and video game industry. For a list of schools in the United States that offer degrees and course work in computer and video game design and programming, visit http://www.igda.org/breakingin/resource_schools.php.

Competition for all types of programming jobs is increasing and will limit the opportunities of those people with less than a bachelor's degree.

Certification or Licensing

No specific certification is available for graphics programmers. General computer-related certifications are available from the Institute for Certification of Computing Professionals, whose address is listed at the end of this article. Although it is not required, certification may boost your attractiveness to employers during the job search.

Other Requirements

Successful graphics programmers need a high degree of reasoning ability, patience, and persistence, as well as an aptitude for mathematics and an artistic eye. They should also have strong writing and speaking skills, so that they can communicate effectively with coworkers and supervisors.

In the computer and video game industry, the work can be stressful, unpredictable, and demanding, so flexibility, enthusiasm, and a love for computer and video games are especially important.

EXPLORING

If you are interested in becoming a graphics programmer in the computer and video game industry, it is a good idea to start early and get some hands-on experience operating and programming a computer. One of the most obvious (and fun) ways to become familiar with the various genres and products of the computer and video game industry is to play lots of different types of computer and video games.

A trip to the local library or bookstore is likely to turn up books on computer programming in general, as well as computer and video game programming. Joining a computer club and reading professional magazines are other ways to become more familiar with this career field. In addition, you should explore the Internet, a great source of information about computer-related careers and the computer and video game industry. One source you might want to check out is *Computer Graphics Quarterly,* a publication of the Special Interest Group on Computer Graphics. You can read back issues of this publication online at http://www.siggraph.org/publications. You also might want to read the online publication *Breaking In: Preparing For Your Career in Games,* which is available at the International Game Developers Association's website, http://www.igda.org/breakingin. The publication offers an overview of programming careers, profiles of workers in the field, and other resources. Student membership in the association is also available.

Another way to gain experience is to visit a company that produces computer and video games and make an appointment to talk with one of the graphics programmers on the staff. You can also contact the computer science department of a local university to get more information about the field. It may be possible to speak with a faculty member whose specialty is computer graphics, or to sit in on a computer graphics class.

If you are interested in the artistic applications of graphics, get involved with artistic projects at school, like theater set design, poster and banner design for extracurricular activities, and yearbook or literary magazine design.

EMPLOYERS

Graphics programmers in the computer and video game industry typically work for small, independent game development studios, large computer and video game publishers, or manufacturers of the various computer and video game platforms. These companies are usually located in major cities, especially on the East and West Coasts.

Graphics programmers in general are employed throughout the United States. Opportunities are best in large cities and suburbs where business and industry are active. Graphics programmers who develop software systems work for software manufacturers, many of which are in central California. There is also a concentration of software manufacturers in Boston, Chicago, and Atlanta. Programmers who adapt and tailor the software to meet specific needs of clients are employed around the country by the end users. Graphics programmers can also work in service centers that furnish computer time and software to businesses. Agencies, called job shops, employ programmers on short-term contracts. Self-employed graphics programmers can also work as consultants to small companies that cannot afford to employ full-time programmers.

STARTING OUT

You can look for an entry-level programming position in the computer and video game industry in the same way as most other jobs; there is no special or standard point of entry into the field. Individuals with the necessary qualifications should apply directly to companies or agencies that have announced job openings through a school placement office, an employment agency, or the classified ads. As employers become increasingly selective about new hires and seek to hold down the costs of in-house training, internships in computer programming are a great opportunity—not only for on-the-job experience, but also for a possible position after graduation from college.

Any previous experience with writing code for games is worth mentioning on your resume, cover letter, and in interviews. Even if it was for a school project, or something done on your own time for fun, it still counts as experience. It shows what you are capable of doing as well as your potential, demonstrates your motivation, and may help you get your foot in the door at a game company.

One thing to keep in mind when looking for employment in the computer and video game industry is geographical location. While there are game companies in most major cities, most are located in cities on the East or West Coasts, in cities such as San Francisco, Seattle, and New York. You may need to consider relocating to boost your chances of finding a job in the computer and video game industry.

ADVANCEMENT

Programmers are often ranked by such terms as *entry-level, associate, junior, or senior programmers*. These titles are based on education, experience, and level of responsibility. After programmers have attained the highest available programming rank, they can choose to make other career moves in order to advance further. Some graphics programmers may wish to become a *lead programmer*. These programmers typically are in charge of a group of programmers working together on a computer game. In addition to being top-notch programmers, they also need to know how to manage a team of programmers (including those with specialties other than graphics programming), deal with upper-level management, and interact with other departments that contribute to the development of a game. These programmers need to have excellent interpersonal skills and enjoy motivating others to perform hard work and strive for excellence. Other management options a programmer might choose to pursue include director, vice president, or other upper-level administrative positions in the computer and video game industry. However, as the level of management responsibilities increases, the amount of technical work performed decreases, so management positions are not for everyone.

Because technology changes so rapidly, programmers must continuously update their training by taking courses sponsored by their employers or software vendors. For skilled workers who keep up to date with the latest technology, the prospects for advancement are good. As employers increasingly contract out programming jobs, more opportunities should arise for experienced programmers with expertise in specific areas to work as consultants.

In general, programming provides a solid background in the computer industry. Experienced programmers enjoy a wide variety of possibilities for career advancement in many computer-related fields.

EARNINGS

According to the National Association of Colleges and Employers, starting salary offers in computer programming averaged $45,558 a year in 2003. The U.S. Department of Labor reports that median annual earnings of computer programmers were $60,290 in 2002. The lowest paid 10 percent earned less than $35,080; the highest 10 percent earned more than $96,860.

Programmers who work as independent consultants earn high salaries, but their salaries may not be regular. Overall, those who work for private industry earn the most.

Graphics programmers usually receive full benefits, such as health insurance, paid vacation, and sick leave.

WORK ENVIRONMENT

Most graphics programmers work with state-of-the-art equipment. They may work alone or as part of a team and often consult with the end users of the graphics program, as well as engineers and other specialists. They usually put in eight to 12 hours a day and work a 40- to 60-hour week. To meet deadlines or finish rush projects, they may work evenings and weekends and average 65 to 80 hours of work a week. At some companies, programmers sometimes find themselves working more than 24 hours at a time, so the office areas are set up with sleeping couches and other areas where employees can relax. Due to long workdays, deadline pressure, and job instability, the computer and video game industry can be a stressful environment in which to work.

Graphics programmers usually work in one primary location but sometimes travel to attend seminars, conferences, and trade shows. Programmers who work for software manufacturers may need to travel to assist current clients in their work or to solicit new customers for the software by demonstrating and discussing the product with potential buyers.

OUTLOOK

Overall, the U.S. Department of Labor predicts that employment for computer programmers is expected to increase about as fast as the average through 2012. The department notes that the demand for computer specialists in general should be strong over the next decade. However, the employment rate for programmers is predicted to be slower than other areas of computer science. Technological developments have made it easier to write basic code, eliminating some of the need for programmers to do this work. More sophisticated software has allowed more and more end users to design, write, and implement their own programs. As a result, many of the programming functions are transferred to other types of workers. In addition, programmers will continue to face increasing competition from international programming businesses where work can be contracted out at a lower cost.

However, the specialty of graphics programming should still have a promising future. As more applications for computer graphics are explored and businesses find ways to use graphics in their everyday operations, graphics programmers will be in demand. Since the field of graphics programming in the computer and video game industry is constantly changing, programmers should stay abreast of the latest technology to remain competitive.

FOR MORE INFORMATION

For industry information, contact
Entertainment Software Association
1211 Connecticut Avenue, NW, #600
Washington, DC 20036
Email: esa@theesa.com
http://www.theesa.com

Gamasutra
600 Harrison Street, 3rd Floor
San Francisco, CA 94107
Tel: 415-947-6206
http://www.gamasutra.com

For career advice and industry information, contact
International Game Developers Association
600 Harrison Street, 6th Floor
San Francisco, CA 94107
Tel: 415-947-6235
Email: info@igda.org
http://www.igda.org

For information on careers and education, student memberships, and the student newsletter looking.forward, *contact*
IEEE Computer Society
1730 Massachusetts Avenue, NW
Washington, DC 20036-1992
Tel: 202-371-0101
Email: membership@computer.org
http://www.computer.org

For information on certification, contact
Institute for Certification of Computing Professionals
2350 East Devon Avenue, Suite 115
Des Plaines, IL 60018-4610
Email: office@iccp.org
http://www.iccp.org

For information on membership, conferences, and publications, contact ACM SIGGRAPH.
Special Interest Group on Computer Graphics
Association for Computing Machinery
1515 Broadway, 17th Floor
New York, NY 10036
Tel: 800-342-6626
http://www.siggraph.org

For a historical timeline of computer graphics and animation, visit
CGI Historical Timeline
http://accad.osu.edu/~waynec/history/timeline.html

Hardware Engineers

OVERVIEW

Computer and video game *hardware engineers* design, build, and test computer hardware (such as computer chips and circuit boards) and computer systems used in making the various platforms for video games. They also work with peripheral devices, such as joysticks and game paddles. Computer and video game hardware engineers are typically employed by the manufacturers of the various game platforms/systems. Most hardware engineers have a degree in computer science or engineering or equivalent computer background. There are approximately 74,000 computer hardware engineers employed in many industries in the United States.

HISTORY

The general field of computer hardware engineers began as a specialty of electrical engineering. Today, many individuals interested in a career in the computer and video game industry turn to computer hardware engineering. The need for computer and video game hardware engineers began in the early 1970s with the hardware engineers focusing on large, coin-operated arcade games. For home use, hardware engineers developed dedicated consoles—computer and video game consoles that only played one game. Shortly thereafter, hardware engineers expanded console technology, allowing game players to play many different games on one console through the use of game cartridges. In the late 1980s, small, handheld games developed by hardware engineers were very popular. The next big platform for game playing was the personal computer—PC and Macs. Game developers realized the virtually limitless options to designing a game to play on a computer.

Hardware engineers made advancements in console development, however, and consoles have continued to remain viable gaming options in the marketplace, along with computers. Like computers, consoles now play games on CDs and DVDs. Hardware engineers also made strides with game-playing peripheral technology for consoles and computers, moving from simple game paddles and joysticks to complex game controllers and memory cards, which allow game players to save games and personal settings, taking them along wherever they play games.

THE JOB

Computer and video game hardware engineers work with the physical components of game platforms. Platforms come in many shapes and sizes: coin-operated arcade games; computers, which also use different operating systems and come in many different technical configurations; video game consoles, such as the Xbox, GameCube, and PlayStation 2; and handheld devices, such as Game Boy. The physical components of a platform include CPUs (computer processing units), motherboards, chipsets, video cards, cooling units, disk drives, storage devices, network cards, and all the components that connect them, down to wires, nuts, and bolts. Computer and video game hardware engineers also work on peripherals, such as keyboards, monitors or other visual displays, mice, track balls, joysticks, game paddles, and audio systems.

Computer and video game hardware engineers design components and create prototypes of platforms to test. They use program tools, such as computer-aided design (CAD), to help them create new products. CAD programs are often used with computer-aided manufacturing (CAM) programs to produce three-dimensional drawings that can easily be altered or manipulated, and direct the actual production of hardware components. They assemble the parts using fine hand tools, soldering irons, and microscopes. Parts are reworked and developed through multiple testing procedures. Once a final design is completed, hardware engineers oversee the manufacture and installation of parts. When a working model of a platform is completed, a typical game may be played on it to determine if there are any incompatibility issues that need to be addressed with the hardware.

Hardware engineers in the computer and video game industry typically work for the manufacturers of the various game platforms. They may work as part of a team of specialists who use elements of science, math, and electronics to improve existing technology or implement solutions. They may also work with additional industry personnel, such as game designers, programmers, and technical support team members to ensure that the platform supports the intended games, and that any incompatibility issues or bugs brought to the attention of technical support are addressed.

REQUIREMENTS

High School

You should take as many courses in computers, electronics, and programming as you can to prepare for this career. Coursework in math and physics will also be beneficial. Speech and writing classes will help you to be able to communicate effectively with coworkers and clients.

Postsecondary Training

Computer hardware engineers need at least a bachelor's degree in computer engineering or electrical engineering; some employment opportunities might require a master's or Ph.D. in computer science or engineering. For a list of accredited four-year computer engineering programs, contact the Accreditation Board for Engineering and Technology.

College studies might include such computer science courses as computer architecture, systems design, chip design, microprocessor design, and network architecture, in addition to a heavy concentration of math and science classes.

Certification or Licensing

Not all computer professionals are certified. The deciding factor seems to be whether or not an employer requires it. Many companies offer tuition reimbursement, or incentives, to those who earn certification. Certification is available in a variety of specialties. The Institute for Certification of Computing Professionals offers the associate computing professional designation for those new to the field and the certified computing professional designation for those with at least 48 months of full-time professional level work in computer-based information systems. Certification is considered by many to be a measure of industry knowledge as well as leverage when negotiating salary.

Other Requirements

Hardware engineers in the computer and video game industry need a broad knowledge of and experience with computer systems and

A hardware engineer makes repairs to equipment in a computer server room. *(Getty Images)*

technologies, especially with games and platforms. You need strong problem-solving and analysis skills and good interpersonal skills. Patience, self-motivation, and flexibility are important. Often, a number of projects are worked on simultaneously, so the ability to multitask is important. Because of rapid technological advances in the computer field, continuing education is a must.

EXPLORING

Ask your computer teacher or guidance counselor to set up an information interview or job-shadowing experience with a hardware engineer You can also talk to your high school computer teacher for more information on the career.

Try to learn as much as possible about computers and computer software. You can learn about new developments by reading trade magazines and talking to other computer users. You also can join computer clubs and perform research on the Internet for information about working in this field.

EMPLOYERS

Computer and video hardware engineers are usually employed by the manufacturers of the various game platforms and peripherals. They are located primarily on the West Coast (in Washington and California) and in Asia.

Hardware engineers outside of the computer and video game industry are employed in nearly every industry, with jobs available nationwide.

STARTING OUT

Education and solid work experience will open industry doors. Though a bachelor's degree is a minimum requirement for most corporate giants, some companies, smaller ones especially, will hire based largely on work experience and practical training. Many computer professionals employed in the computer and video game industry for some time do not have traditional electrical engineering or computer science degrees, but rather moved up on the basis of their work record. However, if you aspire to a management position, then a college degree is usually a necessity.

Large computer companies aggressively recruit on campus armed with signing bonuses and other incentives. Employment opportunities are posted in newspaper want ads daily, with some papers devoting a separate section to computer-related positions. The Internet offers a wealth of employment information plus several sites for browsing job openings, or to post your resume. Most companies maintain a Web page where they post employment opportunities or solicit resumes.

ADVANCEMENT

Many companies hire new grads to work as junior engineers. Problem-solving skills and the ability to implement solutions is a big part of this entry-level job. With enough work experience, junior engineers can move into positions that focus on a particular area in the computer and video game industry, such as platform components or peripherals. Landing a senior-level engineering position is possible after considerable work experience and study. Aspiring hardware engineers should hone their computer skills to the highest level through continuing education, certification, or even advanced graduate study. Many high-level engineers hold a master's degree or better.

Some computer professionals working on the technical side of the industry opt to switch over to the marketing side of the business. Advancement opportunities here may include positions in product management or sales.

Mobile Gaming

Mobile gaming is one of the most popular game-playing methods (along with online gaming) in the industry today. Several types of hardware are involved in mobile gaming, including:

- **Cell Phones.** Almost all new cell phones offer game-playing options. Cell phone games are much less expensive and time-consuming to produce. A cell phone game can be made for as little as $10,000 to $20,000 in three months. Conversely, a typical PlayStation game might cost $5 million and take two or three years to develop.

- **Personal Digital Assistants (PDAs).** The PDAs of the past were fine for *Solitaire* or other basic games, but the newest PDAs offer better graphics, screen resolution, and sound, as well as improved game controls.

- **Mobile Game Platforms (MGP).** Handheld game systems such as Game Boy have been immensely popular for several years. And like cell phone games, MGP games require far less money ($100,000 or less) and time (approximately three months) to create than conventional games.

Source: *Animation World Magazine*

EARNINGS

Computer and video game hardware engineers are classified as computer hardware engineers. The *Occupational Outlook Handbook* reports that median annual earnings of computer hardware engineers were $72,150 in 2002. Salaries ranged from less than $46,190 to more than $114,880. Starting salary offers in 2003 for bachelor's degree candidates in computer engineering averaged $51,343, according to a survey by the National Association of Colleges and Employers. Master's degree candidates averaged $64,200.

Job perks, besides the usual benefit package of insurance, vacation, sick time, and profit sharing, may include stock options, continuing education or training, tuition reimbursement, flexible hours, and child care or other on-site services.

WORK ENVIRONMENT

Most hardware engineers in the computer and video game industry work 40- to 50-hour weeks, or more, depending on the project to which they are assigned. Weekend work is common with some positions. Contrary to popular perceptions, hardware engineers do not spend their workdays cooped up in their offices. Instead, they spend the majority of their time meeting, planning, and working with various staff members from different levels of management and technical expertise. Since it takes numerous workers to take a project from start to finish, team players are in high demand.

OUTLOOK

Computer and video game hardware engineers are classified as computer hardware engineers. Employment in computer hardware engineering will grow more slowly than average through 2012, according to the *Occupational Outlook Handbook*. The number of people earning computer engineering or related degrees has increased rapidly over the past several years, reducing shortages of hardware engineers. Additionally, foreign competition and increased productivity at U.S. companies will limit opportunities for hardware engineers. In addition to new jobs openings, other positions will be available as current computer professionals leave the industry due to retirement or other reasons.

FOR MORE INFORMATION

For a list of accredited programs in computer engineering, contact
**Accreditation Board for Engineering
and Technology (ABET)**
111 Market Place
Suite 1050
Baltimore, MD 21202-4012
Tel: 410-347-7700
http://www.abet.org

For information regarding the computer industry, career opportunities as a computer engineer, or the association's membership requirements, contact
Association for Computing Machinery
1515 Broadway
New York, NY 10036
Tel: 800-342-6626
Email: acmhelp@acm.org
http://www.acm.org

For information on a career in computer engineering, computer scholarships, and the student newsletter looking.forward, contact
IEEE Computer Society
1730 Massachusetts Avenue, NW
Washington, DC 20036-1992
Tel: 1-202-371-0101
http://www.computer.org

For information on certification, contact
Institute for Certification of Computing Professionals
2350 East Devon Avenue, Suite 115
Des Plaines, IL 60018-4610
Email: office@iccp.org
http://www.iccp.org

For computer and video game industry information, contact
Entertainment Software Association
1211 Connecticut Avenue, NW, #600
Washington, DC 20036
Email: esa@theesa.com
http://www.theesa.com

Gamasutra
600 Harrison Street, 3rd Floor
San Francisco, CA 94107
Tel: 415-947-6206
http://www.gamasutra.com

For comprehensive information about careers in electrical engineering and computer science, visit
Sloan Career Cornerstone Center
http://careercornerstone.org

Intellectual Property Lawyers

OVERVIEW

Intellectual property lawyers in the computer and video game industry focus on the protection of creative thought. Intellectual property (IP) lawyers may work with copyrights to protect works their clients have authored; trademarks to protect brand names and symbols associated with their clients' businesses; and patents to protect their clients' inventions and discoveries. IP attorneys may also work with companies to protect their trade secrets. IP lawyers in the computer and video game industry have been kept busy with the explosion of new games and platforms. It is their job to protect emerging new ideas and creations, such as a new game platform, a new game engine, or a new computer and video game design. According to the Franklin Pierce Law Center, the United States is the largest producer of intellectual property in the world.

HISTORY

The concept of intellectual property is not a recent development—people have sought help to protect their ideas since the 1700s. Unfortunately, in the past both lawyers and clients were often frustrated in their attempts to gain support for patents and copyrights in court. The country as a whole, the court system, and Congress were intent on not allowing monopolies to gain control of innovative products or ideas. This fear of monopolization caused the patent holder to get little if any help or protection from the government. Within the past 20 years, however, Congress and judges have started to see innovative ideas and products as valuable for our trade status in the international market.

Attitudes are not the only things that have changed. Compared to the earliest years of inventions, innovative ideas, and patent seeking, huge amounts of intellectual property are now created and need protection daily. Intellectual property in the computer and video game industry now includes music, computer software, written documents like user manuals, programming code, game engines, graphics and much more.

This boom in intellectual property and its need for protection have increased the demand for IP lawyers. Previously, IP law was a smaller segment of a law firm's business, so it was hired out to smaller boutique-type law firms. Now major law firms, game development studios, computer and video game publishers, and manufacturers of the various computer and video game platforms have entire teams in-house to meet the demands of intellectual law.

THE JOB

Intellectual property lawyers in the computer and video game industry work with a wide variety of clients—from an individual programmer or game designer, to the highest level of management of a large game publisher. Those who work for corporations are usually in-house counsels concerned with decisions affecting the use of intellectual property within the company—common examples include game design, game engines, programming code, music and sound effects, graphics, platforms, and any technological discoveries. A video game itself is an example of intellectual property, but it also comprises many different elements that are also examples of intellectual property, and which might be owned by more than one person, group, or company. The most recognized categories of intellectual property are copyrights, trademarks, patents, and trade secrets.

Copyrights initially existed to protect "original works of authorship." This includes works of literature, music, and art. Copyright is now one of the most common forms of intellectual property in the computer and video game industry. Using a finished computer game as an example, the game itself can be copyrighted. Many other aspects of the game can be copyrighted as well, including the game plot, all of the code used in the game, and the musical components of the game.

Trademark rights involve the right to protect name recognition with the public. Trademarks can be many things, including the game name and any logo associated with it, names of characters in the game, and any unique weapons found in the game.

Patents are perhaps the least-used example of intellectual property in the computer and video game industry. Patents may be granted for the invention of something that is new, useful, and original. Editing or control functions, program languages, and core proprietary technology are examples of the aspects of a video game that may be patented.

Trade secrets are information that gives a company an advantage over their competition that doesn't fit into the other three categories. Examples of trade secrets include object, source, and machine code; techniques or methods used to create special effects in a game; and business or marketing plans for a computer and video game company.

IP lawyers in the computer and video game industry have the task of protecting a client's creative interests, whether those interests are to patent a new product, or to ensure that a copyright hasn't been infringed upon. IP lawyers may work in all areas of intellectual property law; however, many lawyers specialize in copyright, patent, trademark, or licensing law. Whichever area the IP attorney focuses on, some job duties are the same across the board. One of the IP lawyer's main tasks is to counsel clients. Usually this counseling concerns whether the intellectual property can be copyrighted, patented, or trademarked; the best method of protection for the individual property; and whether the product or idea being discussed will infringe on someone else's copyright, patent, or trademark. They are often called upon to review advertising copy, press releases, and other official documents to ensure that there are no intellectual property problems. Another major task for an IP lawyer is the drafting of legal documents, such as patent applications and licensing agreements. They may also help their clients choose an Internet domain name or a trademark.

The IP lawyer also serves clients by being their advocate before administrative bodies and courts. The IP lawyer's goal is to secure the rights of the client and then protect those rights if others violate them. Conversely, if the IP lawyer's client is accused of violating someone else's intellectual property rights, the IP lawyer defends the client.

If a client believes his or her rights to intellectual property have been infringed upon, the IP attorney must try to prove that someone else has taken or used the client's intellectual property without consent. On the other hand, if a client is accused of infringing on another's intellectual property rights, the lawyer must try to prove that the

Two intellectual property
lawyers research a trademark
infringement case in a law library.
(Robert Rathe, MIRA)

item in question didn't deserve a copyright, patent, or trademark in
the first place or that the protection is invalid. Although lawsuits are
commonplace today, most IP lawyers consider litigation to be the last
step and try to settle differences outside the courtroom.

REQUIREMENTS

High School
Because intellectual property often deals with creations in the scientific, engineering, literary, and music worlds, a background in any of
those areas will be helpful. If you are interested in working as an IP
lawyer in the computer and video game industry, you should take as
many computer classes as you can while in high school. Take courses in business, accounting, English, and government as well.

Postsecondary Training
As in other areas of law, IP lawyers most often complete an undergraduate degree and then graduate from law school. For most types
of intellectual property law, the undergraduate degree does not
have to have a special focus. The exception to that is patent law. If
you want to become a patent lawyer, you should major in science,
engineering, or physics. Other technology-related courses will also
be helpful.

To apply to almost any law school, you must first pass the Law School Admission Test (LSAT). The LSAT is an aptitude test that is used to predict how successful an individual will be in law school. Most law schools teach courses in intellectual property law, but some have IP sections and degrees, such as Columbia University School of Law, Franklin Pierce Law Center, and George Mason University Law School.

Certification or Licensing

After graduating from law school, you will be eligible to take the bar exam in any state. After passing the bar, you will be sworn in as an attorney and will then be eligible to practice law. Patent attorneys who practice patent law before the United States Patent Office must go a step further and obtain additional certification. Would-be patent lawyers must pass the patent bar exam. According to the American Bar Association, you must hold a bachelor's degree in engineering or one of the sciences, hold a bachelor's degree in another subject, or have passed the Engineer in Training (EIT) test in order to be eligible to take the patent bar exam.

Other Requirements

IP lawyers should have excellent written and oral communication skills. In fact, the American Bar Foundation says a recent survey shows that law firms are more interested in these skills than the overall legal knowledge of the interviewee. Also, having command of foreign languages is crucial because IP lawyers work with products and ideas in international markets. IP lawyers in the computer and video game industry should have a good understanding of computer and video games and their components.

EXPLORING

IP law in the computer and video game industry is a perfect career for someone who is interested in both science and technology of games and law. Because of this duality, you can explore the career by focusing on the legal side or on the science/technology side. To get experience on the legal side, seek summer jobs and internships with law offices where you live. You may be able to get a part-time job as a legal assistant. Any experience you can get writing technical or legal documents can also help, so don't rule out temporary jobs in any kind of business office. Also check out your local business college for special prelaw programs that offer introductory law courses to the public. If you can't get any hands-on experience right away, ask your guidance counselor for help in setting up a tour of a local law office or arranging for an interview with a law professional. To get experience in the science/technology side in the computer and video game industry, you can ask for a tour of a computer and video game company or arrange for an interview with a professional in the industry. You can also join your school's computer club and check out computer and game publications at your local library and on the Internet.

EMPLOYERS

Intellectual property lawyers are in high demand with many types of employers in the computer and video game industry. IP lawyers are employed at law firms, hardware manufacturing corporations, design studios, and software publishers. IP lawyers may also own their own businesses.

The main employer of IP attorneys outside of the computer and video game industry is the United States Patent and Trademark Office (USPTO), which is part of the Department of Commerce. The USPTO employs lawyers as trademark examiners, patent examiners, and more. Other departments in the government that employ IP lawyers include the Departments of Defense, Interior, Justice, and Energy. IP lawyers can also find employment in the United States Copyright Office.

Although IP lawyers are in high demand all over the country, most work in large cities where the major corporations are headquartered. Other hot spots for IP lawyers include Washington, D.C., because of the government agencies located there, and the West Coast—like the Silicon Valley area in California, and in and around Seattle—because of its concentration of computer and video game–related industry.

STARTING OUT

As in any area of law, internships and clerkships are usually the path to a quality job. For those interested in patent law specifically, applying for a clerkship in the United States Court of Appeals for the Federal Court in Washington, D.C., is a great way to gain experience. To apply for an unpaid, part-time internship during law school or soon after graduation, you should write directly to the court about six months in advance. To gain a full-time, paid clerkship position, law students should inquire sometime before the end of their second year. You can also apply for clerkships and internships with law firms. Another way to break into the IP law field is to get a job at the

USPTO. Working directly with patents will put you in a better position for an IP job later in your career.

ADVANCEMENT

Most IP lawyers start out with internships and clerkships at firms or courts. In law firms or large corporate offices in the computer and video game industry, IP lawyers start out as low-rung associates and then advance as their experience and track records allow. Associates with successful reputations and many years of experience can become partners in the law firm or advance within the legal department at a computer and video game company. Whether in corporations, government agencies, or law firms, most IP lawyers, like other types of lawyers, are given more high-profile cases and more important clients as they become more experienced.

EARNINGS

According to the American Intellectual Property Law Association, the average salary for an IP attorney in corporate offices and patent firms is $119,000 per year. Inexperienced IP lawyers can expect to make between $80,000 and $85,000, and those with the most experience and success will earn more than $180,000 per year. The median income for partners in private law firms is over $200,000 per year, while associates' salary is about $77,000. IP lawyers who own their own practices usually make $100,000 per year while salaries for those who work in law firms and corporations average slightly higher.

Almost all corporations, firms, and government agencies provide medical insurance, vacation, sick days, and holidays. Partners in large firms can expect other perks as well, including company cars, spending allowances, bonuses, and more depending on the firm.

WORK ENVIRONMENT

IP attorneys, like lawyers in other areas, have heavy workloads and work long hours. IP lawyers employed in law firms and in computer and video game companies may spend hours poring over documents with few breaks. Many law firms have weekly goals for their lawyers that include the number of hours billed to the client. Some of these goals can be extremely demanding. Most of the lawyer's time is spent indoors meeting with clients, researching, or arguing in court. Depending on their position in the company or firm, IP lawyers may lead a team of lawyers or supervise a group of paralegals and associates.

OUTLOOK

The outlook for intellectual property law is promising. This field is relatively new and the demand for IP professionals doesn't show signs of slowing. The growth of the computer industry and the Internet have provided a great amount of work for IP lawyers. As new computer software and online media enters the market, IP lawyers will be needed to protect it. According to the American Bar Association, even if other markets that use the services of lawyers are softened by recession, the demand for IP lawyers will remain high. Because there will always be a need to protect the creative resources of the people, there will also be a need for IP lawyers.

FOR MORE INFORMATION

For information on all areas of law, law schools, the bar exam, and career guidance, contact
   American Bar Association
   541 North Fairbanks Court
   Chicago, IL 60611
   Tel: 800-285-2221
   Email: askaba@abanet.org
   http://www.abanet.org

To read the publications What Is a Patent, a Trademark and a Copyright? *and* Careers in IP Law, *visit the AIPLA website.*
   American Intellectual Property Law Association
   2001 Jefferson Davis Highway, Suite 203
   Arlington, VA 22202
   Tel: 703-415-0780
   Email: aipla@aipla.org
   http://www.aipla.org

For computer and video game industry information, contact
   Entertainment Software Association
   1211 Connecticut Avenue, NW, #600
   Washington, DC 20036
   Email: esa@theesa.com
   http://www.theesa.com

Gamasutra
600 Harrison Street, 3rd Floor
San Francisco, CA 94107
Tel: 415-947-6206
http://www.gamasutra.com

For information about IP law and degree programs, contact
Franklin Pierce Law Center
Two White Street
Concord, NH 03301
Tel: 603-228-1541
Email: admissions@piercelaw.edu
http://www.fplc.edu

For career advice and industry information, contact
International Game Developers Association
600 Harrison Street, 6th Floor
San Francisco, CA 94107
Tel: 415-947-6235
Email: info@igda.org
http://www.igda.org

For information on patent law, contact
National Association of Patent Practitioners
4680-18-i Monticello Avenue
PMB 101
Williamsburg, VA 23188
Tel: 800-216-9588
Email: napp@napp.org
http://www.napp.org

For information about IP, job opportunities, and recent press releases, contact the USPTO. Their website offers a link designed specifically for creative students interested in invention and includes contest information.
United States Patent and Trademark Office
Crystal Plaza 3, Room 2C02
PO Box 1450
Alexandria, VA 22313-1450
Tel: 800-786-9199
Email: usptoinfo@uspto.gov
http://www.uspto.gov

INTERVIEW

Jim Charne is a lawyer in Santa Monica, California, who represents developers, designers, and other creative professionals in the game industry. He is a past president and executive director of the Academy of Interactive Arts and Sciences, writes a monthly column that appears on the Web at http://www.igda.org/columns/lastwords, and has been a lawyer for 24 years. Mr. Charne spoke with the editors of Careers in Focus: Computer & Video Game Design *about his career and legal issues affecting the game industry.*

Q. What made you want to focus on intellectual property (IP) law?

A. I originally worked in the record business and became interested in intellectual property, which is the core of that business. Ownership of catalogs of master recordings gives record companies value. Ownership of song copyrights gives music publishers value. When I started, intellectual property was a sleepy little specialty, but to me it had a direct link to creativity and artistry—two areas of great personal interest.

In law school, I was very fortunate to study copyright under Seymour Peyser, a wonderful man who was a prosecutor at the Nuremburg trials after WWII, later served as General Counsel of United Artists Corporation, and was a longtime partner at Phillips Nizer Benjamin Krim and Ballon in New York. I took copyright at the time we were transitioning from the 1909 Copyright Act to the 1976 Act (which is still current). It was a time of great turmoil in the field, and Professor Peyser brought his experience and enthusiasm to the subject. He inspired me to want to work in the area.

Q. What are your primary and secondary job duties?

A. I am in the private practice of law. I primarily represent clients on the talent side. This means I represent game developers, designers, composers, and other individual talent. I provide counsel and representation in all aspects of a business, or for an individual providing services in the creation of game content. This means I get involved in company formation, shareholder or partnership agreements, collaboration agreements, setting of employment practices and policies, negotiation of commercial leases, licensing, work-for-hire technical and creative services agreements, software development deals, financing, copyright registration, trademark prosecution, and any other types of transactions that arise out of a software business. I am also involved in informal mediation of disputes, and from time to time, litigation.

Another part of my practice is to be a sounding board for clients to discuss issues that arise. One synonym for "lawyer" is "counsel." I provide counsel for clients on a wide range of issues and questions.

Q. What is your work environment like?

A. I am a sole practitioner so my work environment is what makes me comfortable. My office is in Santa Monica, California. I am in a second floor walk-up, four blocks from the beach, and I can open all my windows to enjoy the ocean breeze. I share the suite with my wife who is a writer and professor of screenwriting at UCLA Film School. We have a large sitting room with a conference table that can easily seat 10. We have sofas and chairs for client conferences and a kitchen.

Q. Do you travel often for your job?

A. I travel to industry events, and find myself in Europe once or twice each year. I am fortunate that the game business and my practice are international in scope. I represent clients who are located around the United States, in Canada, Europe, and Asia. It is important to have a personal relationship with clients and with other professionals in the industry. As a lawyer, I make "house calls." I try to visit clients whenever possible in their work places.

Q. In addition to your law degree, what type of specialized training did you receive to prepare for this career?

A. My undergraduate major was communications arts with an area of concentration in radio-TV-film. When I graduated from the University of Wisconsin, my first job was with CBS Records (the predecessor of Sony Music) in radio promotion and product marketing/product management. I went to law school at night for four years while I was advancing in my career at CBS in New York. When I graduated, I left CBS and spent one year as a lawyer on the staff of Arista Records. I then started a general entertainment, but music-industry focused, private practice in Manhattan.

The first exposure I had to the game industry was through a friend who was head of Atco Records. Atco was owned by Warner Communications, who also owned Atari. I heard over and over how fast this business was growing, how profitable Atari was, and how it kept getting bigger and bigger (we all know how that story ended). That got me interested in the possibilities of using computers as entertainment devices.

One day I saw an ad in the Sunday *New York Times* Business Section from Activision (then a private company in Mountain View, California) looking for an East Coast–based producer. I thought that would be the best way to learn the game business, so I applied. After multiple interviews, I was hired and spent nearly three years managing all East Coast game development for Activision. Along the way, I took the New Jersey bar exam and witnessed firsthand the collapse of the Atari 2600 video game business (no one had yet figured out how to do hardware transitions in the game business). But during that three year period, I decided this is what I really wanted to do.

Q. What are some of the pros and cons of your job?

A. Pros: Interesting clients and interesting projects. Games people are among the smartest creative and business people around.

Cons: Difficult issues, difficult negotiations, and tight deadlines (including the 24/7 nature of deadlines).

Q. What personal qualities do IP lawyers need to be successful in the field?

A. First and foremost, you have to be a good lawyer and a good listener. Develop all your lawyerly skills and do not focus on any specialty. Be thorough and detail-oriented. Think before you open your mouth. Never take shortcuts. Always put the client first. Be respectful of your profession, your clients, and the other side. Learn the code of professional responsibility and live up to the meaning and intent, not just the letter. Lawyers have high professional standards, including duties of absolute loyalty, honesty, and confidentiality to their clients. Never forget that.

I attend a regular luncheon at the Beverly Hills Bar Association where ethical issues are discussed. The leader of the program says when a lawyer dies, he or she is buried at six feet, but the coffin sinks lower because of the weight of all the client secrets and confidences the lawyer takes to the grave. For a lawyer in any field, your reputation for integrity is your most important asset.

Q. How does an IP lawyer acquire clients or advertise his or her services to the game industry?

A. I believe Woody Allen said that 90 percent of success in life is just showing up. Attend industry events, get to know people, don't be afraid to volunteer, look for opportunities to contribute to projects, write for publication if you have something to say.

Q. **What are the main IP issues that are affecting the computer and video game industry today?**

A. Ownership and control of game IP; ownership and control of developer tools and technology; ancillary rights to game assets; control of designs and game decisions by third-party content licensors; and, although not necessarily an IP issue, the financing of games for next-generation platforms.

Marketing Research Analysts

OVERVIEW

Marketing research analysts in the computer and video game industry collect, analyze, and interpret data in order to determine potential demand for computer or video games or platforms. By examining the buying habits, wants, needs, and preferences of consumers, research analysts are able to recommend ways to improve products, increase sales, and expand customer bases. There are approximately 155,000 marketing research analysts employed in the United States.

HISTORY

Knowing what customers want and what prices they are willing to pay have always been concerns of manufacturers and producers of goods and services. As industries have grown and competition for consumers of manufactured goods has increased, businesses have turned to marketing research as a way to measure public opinion and assess customer preferences. The computer and video game industry is no different.

Marketing research formally emerged in Germany in the 1920s and in Sweden and France in the 1930s. In the United States, emphasis on marketing research began after World War II. With a desire to study potential markets and gain new customers, U.S. firms hired marketing research specialists, professionals who were able to use statistics and refine research techniques to help companies reach their marketing goals. By the 1980s, research analysts could be found even in a variety of Communist countries, where the quantity of consumer goods being produced was rapidly increasing. Today, the marketing research analyst is a vital part of the marketing team. By conducting studies and analyzing data, research professionals help companies address specific marketing issues and concerns.

Perhaps the first example of market research being put to use in the computer and game industry took place in the early 1970s. Nolan Bushnell released *Computer Space,* a video arcade game. Although based on the popular *Spacewar* game that had been floating around university mainframes for nearly a decade, it was a flop when released to the general public. The problem? The average person found it to be too complicated to play, and therefore not very entertaining. Taking this criticism into account, Bushnell made his next game, *Pong*, considerably simpler to play. The game quickly became popular and was a huge success.

Marketing computer and video game products has become more complicated as the industry continues to evolve and expand. The explosion of games available in different genres (action, adventure, simulation, and strategy, for example) has created specialty markets, each requiring different marketing techniques. Games that play on more than one platform also require different marketing tactics for each potential platform audience. Finally, with more and more companies producing similar games and platforms, the marketing emphasis now is on how to advertise a new product to set it apart from a similar product sold by a competitor, rather than just highlighting the product itself.

THE JOB

Marketing research analysts in the computer and video game industry collect and analyze all kinds of information in order to help companies improve their products, establish or modify sales and distribution policies, and make decisions regarding future plans and directions. In addition, marketing research analysts are responsible for monitoring both in-house studies and off-site research, interpreting results, providing explanations of compiled data, and developing research tools. The emphasis placed on market research varies among computer and video game companies. In some companies, market research plays an enormous role—even dictating entirely which game ideas get developed and which ideas are killed. Other companies use market research in a more supportive role, using the information gathered to fine-tune current games in development or future game proposals.

One area of marketing research focuses on company products and services. In order to determine consumer likes and dislikes, marketing research analysts collect data on brand names, trademarks, product design, and packaging for existing products, items being test-marketed, and those in experimental stages. Analysts also study competing products and services that are already on the market to help game designers develop new products.

In the sales methods and policy area of marketing research, analysts examine firms' sales records and conduct a variety of sales-related studies. For example, information on game or platform sales in various geographical areas is analyzed and compared to previous sales figures, changes in population, and total and seasonal sales volume. By analyzing this data, marketing researchers can identify peak sales periods and recommend ways to target new customers. Such information helps marketers plan future sales campaigns and establish sales quotas and commissions.

Advertising research is closely related to sales research. Studies on the effectiveness of advertising in different parts of the country are conducted and compared to sales records. This research is helpful in planning future advertising campaigns and in selecting the appropriate media to use.

Marketing research that focuses on consumer demand and preferences solicits opinions of the people who use the products or services being considered. Besides actually conducting opinion studies, marketing researchers often design the ways to obtain the information. They write scripts for telephone interviews, develop direct-mail questionnaires and field surveys, and design focus group programs. In addition to these methods, analysts in the computer and video game industry often use communities, affinity groups, chat rooms, and forums to gather opinions and feedback regarding their products, as well as gamers' preferences and habits in general. Communities involve assembling a group by setting up "meeting places" for users of a product to discuss their views and opinions. They can exist as online forums, local gatherings, or a combination of the two. Affinity groups, similar to focus groups, usually involve speaking with die-hard game users and their friends, usually in the gamer's house, to gather information about general gaming preferences. Because many computer and video game users are extremely computer-literate, the Internet is a great resource for market research analysts. Chat rooms and online forums can be monitored by or even established by the market research analysts, and are great places to gather opinions and feedback regarding their products.

Through one or a combination of these studies, market researchers are able to gather information on consumer reaction to the style, design, price, and use of a product. The studies attempt to reveal who uses various products, identify potential customers, or get suggestions for product or service improvement. This information is helpful for forecasting sales, planning design modifications, and determining changes in features.

A number of professionals make up the marketing research team. The *project supervisor* is responsible for overseeing a study from beginning to end. The *statistician* determines the sample size—or the number of people to be surveyed—and compares the number of responses. The project supervisor or statistician, in conjunction with other specialists (such as *demographers* and *psychologists*), often determines the number of interviews to be conducted as well as their locations. *Field interviewers* survey people in various public places, such as shopping malls, office complexes, and popular attractions. *Telemarketers* gather information by placing calls to current or potential customers, to people listed in telephone books, or to those who appear on specialized lists obtained from list houses. Once questionnaires come in from the field, *tabulators* and *coders* examine the data, count the answers, code ambiguous answers, and tally the primary counts. The marketing research analyst then analyzes the returns, writes up the final report, and makes recommendations to the design team and/or management of the computer and video game company.

Marketing research analysts in the computer and video game industry must be thoroughly familiar with the products of the industry. They must also be thoroughly familiar with research techniques and procedures. Sometimes the research problem is clearly defined, and information can be gathered readily. Other times, company executives may know only that a problem exists as evidenced by an unexpected decline in the sales of a game or platform. In these cases, the market research analyst is expected to collect the facts that will aid in revealing and resolving the problem, using some of the many techniques and procedures at his or her disposal.

REQUIREMENTS

High School

Most employers require their marketing research analysts to hold at least a bachelor's degree, so a college preparatory program is advised. Classes in English, marketing, economics, mathematics, psychology, and sociology are particularly important. Courses in computing are especially useful, since a great deal of tabulation and statistical analysis is required in the marketing research field.

Postsecondary Training

A bachelor's degree is essential for careers in marketing research. Majors in marketing, business administration, statistics, computer science, history, or economics provide a good background for most types of research positions. In addition, course work in sociology and psychology is helpful for those who are leaning toward consumer demand and opinion research. Since quantitative skills are important in various types of industrial or analytic research, students interested in these areas should take statistics, econometrics, survey design, sampling theory, and other mathematics courses.

Many employers prefer that a marketing research analyst hold a master's degree as well as a bachelor's degree. A master's of business administration, for example, is frequently required on projects calling for complex statistical and business analysis. Graduate work at the doctorate level is not necessary for most positions, but it is highly desirable for those who plan to become involved in advanced research studies.

Other Requirements

To work in this career, you should be intelligent, detail oriented, and accurate; have the ability to work easily with words and numbers; and be particularly interested in solving problems through data collection and analysis. In addition, you must be patient and persistent, since long hours are often required when working on complex studies.

As part of the market research team, you must be able to work well with others and have an interest in people. The ability to communicate clearly, both orally and in writing, is also important, since you will be responsible for writing up detailed reports on the findings in various studies and presenting recommendations to management.

Many marketing positions in the computer and video game industry require some knowledge of computer games and platforms, and experience in the computer and video game industry.

EXPLORING

You can find many opportunities in high school to learn more about the necessary skills for the field of marketing research in general. For example, experiments in science, problems in student government, committee work, and other school activities provide exposure to situations similar to those encountered by marketing research analysts.

You can also seek part-time employment as a survey interviewer at local marketing research firms. Gathering field data for consumer surveys offers valuable experience through actual contact with both the public and marketing research supervisors. In addition, many companies seek a variety of other employees to code, tabulate, and edit surveys; monitor telephone interviews; and validate the information entered on written questionnaires. You can search for job listings in local newspapers and on the Web or apply directly to research organizations.

Familiarizing yourself with computer and video games is one way to become aware of the industry, and thus the different aspects of a game or platform that a market research analyst might be concerned with. You can also inquire about *beta testing* new computer and video game products. Many companies provide information about beta testing on their websites. As a beta tester, you will be asked to play games currently in development and then critique the product. Your comments are then used to perfect the product before it is released to the general public. Another way to become involved in another aspect of computer and video game industry market research is to participate in *communities*—meeting places for users of a product to discuss their views and opinions. They exist as online forums, local gatherings, or a combination of the two. These communities are frequently focused on one company or a specific product, often set up by the companies themselves to gather opinions and feedback regarding their products.

EMPLOYERS

In the computer and video game industry, marketing research analysts are typically employed by independent game development studios, computer and video game publishers, manufacturers of the various computer and video game platforms, and private research organizations that specialize in this industry. These companies are usually located in major cities, especially on the East and West Coasts. Major entertainment software publishers include Electronic Arts, Nintendo of America, Activision, Atari, Sony, Vivendi Universal, THQ, Take 2 Interactive, Microsoft, and Konami Digital Entertainment-America.

While many marketing research organizations offer a broad range of services, some firms subcontract parts of an overall project out to specialized companies. For example, one research firm may concentrate on product interviews, while another might focus on measuring the effectiveness of product advertising. Similarly, some marketing analysts specialize in one industry, area, or platform.

Although many smaller firms located all across the country outsource studies to marketing research firms, these research firms, along

Books to Read

Adams, Ernest. *Break into the Game Industry: How to Get A Job Making Video Games*. New York: McGraw-Hill Osborne Media, 2003.

Bates, Bob, ed. *Game Developer's Market Guide*. Stamford, Conn.: Premier Press, 2003.

Bethke, Erik. *Game Development and Production*. Plano, Tex.: Wordware Publishing, 2003.

Boer, James R. *Game Audio Programming*. Hingham, Mass.: Charles River Media, 2002.

Champandard, Alex J. *AI Game Development*. Berkeley, Calif.: New Riders, 2003.

Gershenfeld, Alan, Mark Loparco, and Cecilia Barajas. *Game Plan: The Insider's Guide to Breaking in and Succeeding in the Computer and Video Game Business*. New York: St. Martin's Griffin, 2003.

Kent, Steven L. *The Ultimate History of Video Games: From Pong to Pokemon—The Story Behind the Craze That Touched Our Lives and Changed the World*. New York: Prima Lifestyles, 2001.

Kushner, David. *Masters of Doom: How Two Guys Created an Empire and Transformed Pop Culture*. New York: Random House, 2003.

LaMothe, André. *Windows Game Programming for Dummies*. 2nd ed. New York: Wiley, 2002.

Laramee, Francois Dominic, ed. *Secrets of the Game Business*. Hingham, Mass.: Charles River Media, 2003.

Marks, Aaron. *The Complete Guide to Game Audio: For Composers, Musicians, Sound Designers, and Game Developers*. San Francisco, Calif.: CMP Books, 2001.

McCuskey, Mason. *Beginning Game Audio Programming*. Stamford, Conn.: Premier Press, 2003.

Meigs, Tom. *Ultimate Game Design: Building Game Worlds*. New York: McGraw-Hill Osborne Media, 2003.

(continues)

(continued)

Mulligan, Jessica, and Bridgette Patrovsky. *Developing Online Games: An Insider's Guide*. Berkeley, Calif.: New Riders, 2003.

Ray, Sheri Graner. *Gender Inclusive Game Design: Expanding the Market*. Hingham, Mass.: Charles River Media, 2003.

Salisbury, Ashley, and Andre LaMothe. *Game Development Business and Legal Guide*. Stamford, Conn.: Premier Press, 2003.

Zerbst, Stefan. *3D Game Engine Programming*. Stamford, Conn.: Premier Press, 2004.

with most large corporations that employ marketing research analysts, are located in such big cities as New York or Chicago.

In addition to working in the computer and video game industry, marketing research analysts are employed by large corporations, industrial firms, advertising agencies, data collection businesses, and private research organizations that handle local surveys for companies on a contract basis. Approximately 155,000 marketing research analysts are employed in the United States.

STARTING OUT

Students with a graduate degree in marketing research and experience in quantitative techniques have the best chances of landing jobs as marketing research analysts. Since a bachelor's degree in marketing or business is usually not sufficient to obtain such a position, many employees without postgraduate degrees start out as research assistants, trainees, interviewers, or questionnaire editors. In such positions, those aspiring to the job of market research analyst can gain valuable experience conducting interviews, analyzing data, and writing reports. In addition, many marketing positions in the computer and video game industry require some knowledge of computer games and platforms, and experience in the computer and video game industry. Working in computer and video game sales for a year or two is a good way to gain experience.

Use your college placement office and help wanted sections of local newspapers to look for job leads. The Internet is also a good source to use, and websites such as http://www.gamejobs.com, http://www.siia.net, and http://www.gamasutra.com offer information on jobs and employers. Another way to get into the marketing research field is through personal and professional contacts. Names and telephone numbers of potential employers may come from professors, friends, or relatives. Finally, students who have participated in internships or have held marketing research-related jobs on a part-time basis while in school or during the summer may be able to obtain employment at these firms or at similar organizations.

ADVANCEMENT

Most marketing research professionals begin as *junior analysts* or *research assistants*. In these positions, they help in preparing questionnaires and related materials, training survey interviewers, and tabulating and coding survey results. After gaining sufficient experience in these and other aspects of research project development, employees are often assigned their own research projects, which usually involve supervisory and planning responsibilities. A typical promotion path for those climbing the company ladder might be from assistant researcher to marketing research analyst to assistant manager and then to manager of a branch office for a large private research firm. From there, some professionals become market research executives or research directors for industrial or business firms.

Since marketing research analysts learn about all aspects of marketing on the job, some advance by moving to positions in other departments, such as advertising or sales. Depending on the interests and experience of marketing professionals, other areas of employment to which they can advance include data processing, teaching at the university level, statistics, economics, and industrial research and development.

In general, few employees go from starting positions to executive jobs at one company. Advancement often requires changing employers. Therefore, marketing research analysts who want to move up the ranks frequently go from one company to another, sometimes many times during their careers.

EARNINGS

Beginning salaries in marketing research depend on the qualifications of the employee, the nature of the position, and the size of the firm. Interviewers, coders, tabulators, editors, and a variety of other employees usually get paid by the hour and may start at $6 or more per hour. There is no specific salary information available for market research analysts who are employed in the computer and video game industry. According to the U.S. Department of Labor, median annual earnings of market research analysts employed in all industries were $53,810 in 2002. The middle 50 percent earned salaries that ranged from $38,760 to $76,310. Salaries ranged from less than $29,390 to more than $100,160. Experienced analysts working in supervisory positions at large firms can earn even higher earnings. Market research directors earn up to $200,000.

Because most marketing research workers are employed by business or industrial firms, they receive typical fringe benefit packages, including health and life insurance, pension plans, and paid vacation and sick leave.

WORK ENVIRONMENT

Marketing research analysts usually work a 40-hour week. Occasionally, overtime is necessary in order to meet project deadlines. Although they frequently interact with a variety of marketing research team members, analysts also do a lot of independent work, analyzing data, writing reports, and preparing statistical charts. In addition, those employed in the computer and video game industry often have a great deal of interaction with the game and product designers and development staff.

Most marketing research analysts work in offices located at the firm's main headquarters. Analysts working in the computer and video game industry usually have offices at the company that employs them, or they may work from home. Those who supervise interviewers may go into the field to oversee work. In order to attend conferences, meet with clients, or check on the progress of various research studies, many market research analysts find that regular travel is required.

OUTLOOK

The U.S. Department of Labor predicts that employment for marketing research analysts employed in all fields will grow faster than the average through 2012. Increasing competition among computer and video game companies, strong sales of computer and video games (239 million games were sold in 2003, according to the Entertainment Software Association), and a growing awareness of the value of marketing research data will contribute to strong growth for game industry marketing research analysts. Opportunities will be best for those with a master's degree who also have previous experience with computer and video games.

FOR MORE INFORMATION

For career resources and job listings, contact
American Marketing Association
311 South Wacker Drive, Suite 5800
Chicago, IL 60606
Tel: 800-262-1150
Email: info@ama.org
http://www.marketingpower.com

For information on graduate programs in marketing, contact
Council of American Survey Research Organizations
170 North Country Road, Suite 4
Port Jefferson, NY 11777
Tel: 631-928-6954
Email: casro@casro.org
http://www.casro.org

For industry information, contact
Entertainment Software Association
1211 Connecticut Avenue, NW, #600
Washington, DC 20036
Email: esa@theesa.com
http://www.theesa.com

Software and Information Industry Association
1090 Vermont Ave, NW, Sixth Floor
Washington, DC 20005-4095
Tel: 202-289-7442
http://www.siia.net

For comprehensive career information, including Breaking In: Preparing For Your Career in Games, *visit the IGDA website.*
International Game Developers Association
600 Harrison Street, 6th Floor
San Francisco, CA 94107
Phone: 415-947-6235
Email: info@igda.org
http://www.igda.org

For information on education and training, contact
   Marketing Research Association
   1344 Silas Deane Highway, Suite 306
   Rocky Hill, CT 06067-0230
   Tel: 860-257-4008
   Email: email@mra-net.org
   http://www.mra-net.org

Packaging Designers

QUICK FACTS

School Subjects
Art
Computer science

Personal Skills
Artistic
Mechanical/manipulative

Work Environment
Primarily indoors
Primarily one location

Minimum Education Level
Some postsecondary training

Salary Range
$21,600 to $36,630 to
$65,060+

Certification or Licensing
None available

Outlook
Faster than the average

DOT
141

GOE
01.02.03

NOC
N/A

O*NET-SOC
27-1024.00

OVERVIEW

Packaging designers in the computer and video game industry design product packaging and related materials for computer and video game products. They often work with packaging engineers, product managers, and marketing and sales personnel to design packages that not only protect the product but also present it in a manner that is visually pleasing and adds to its marketability.

HISTORY

Historically, there has been a need for people to express themselves creatively through the use of pictures, graphics, and words. This means of expression remains a vital part of today's manufacturing and marketing.

When computer and video games were first developed, their packaging was utilitarian at best—product contents were apt to be sealed in a plain old plastic bag. Soon simple packaging techniques, using cardboard or plastic, were utilized. More elaborate packaging techniques took off when Electronic Arts, a developer and publisher of games, mimicked the packaging used by the music industry: the use of vivid, eye-catching art, and the inclusion of additional product information other than just the requisite instructions. Other companies followed suit and packaged their games in imaginative fashions: one company even packaged its tennis video game in tennis ball canisters! Prevailing retail-marketing principles have since toned down such extravagant packaging designs, as there are simply too many games and console systems competing for a limited amount of shelf space. Tight, uniform design shapes are the key.

Today's packaging designers in the computer and video game industry still use endless amounts of images and colors to advertise and promote their products. Although computers now aid many of today's packaging designers, creativity, imagination, and ingenuity must still drive the artistic process.

THE JOB

Packaging designers in the computer and video game industry usually work for computer and video game publishers, game development studios, manufacturers of the various computer and video game platforms, or for a company that offers package design services. They typically work with a team of employees to design and implement the packaging for products. From a marketing standpoint, packaging design is vital. When faced with a choice of many similar products, consumers often evaluate a product from its package, so the importance of a design making an immediate good impression cannot be overstated in the competitive computer and video game industry.

To get started with a packaging design, the packaging designer typically meets with a team of employees that includes people in the industry such as the game designer, product manager, the packaging engineer, the copywriter, and the marketing manager. They discuss "box and docs"—computer and video game industry lingo for the package and everything that goes in it: "box" refers to the physical packaging; and "docs " refers to everything that goes inside of the package, including the game, user manual, and any other instructions or documentation. Together the team determines the type of package to be produced, safety and storage issues, and the intended market. The package designer must consider all of these factors when designing a package. The package designer must also take into consideration any design elements (such as product pictures, instructions, or a logo) and labeling requirements (ratings information, platform and media specifications, the SKU barcode) that need to be included.

The amount of actual design work a packaging designer needs to do varies from project to project. Philip Travisano is a designer who works for Konami Digital Entertainment-America, one of the largest video game producers in the world. He has worked on more than two dozen different video game packaging designs. Regarding design work for video game packages, Travisano says, "Sometimes I design them from scratch, sometimes I get pre-designed logos and main images and just assemble them in a nice composition."

With all of the necessary considerations in mind, the packaging designer develops one or more packaging designs by using traditional

Game Ratings

Virtually all computer games are rated by the Entertainment Software Rating Board (ESRB), an organization that was established by the Interactive Digital Software Association in 1994. Software publishers voluntarily submit their games to the ESRB for rating. The ESRB does not rate the quality or playability of the games, but, rather, rates each game on its appropriateness for certain age groups.

The ESRB uses the following rating symbols to rate approximately 1,000 games a year.

Rating	Description
EC-Early Childhood	Offers content that would be suitable for ages three and up.
E-Everyone	Offers content that would be suitable for ages six and up. May feature minimal violence and/or mild language.
T-Teen	Offers content that would be suitable for ages 13 and up. May feature mild or strong language, violence, and/or suggestive themes.
M-Mature	Offers content that would be suitable for ages 17 and up. May feature mature sexual themes and/or strong violence and language.
AO-Adults Only	Not intended for persons under the age of 18. May feature graphic depictions of sex and/or violence.
RP-Rating Pending	This refers to a title that has been submitted to the ESRB, but that has not yet been rated.

In 2003 . . .

- 54 percent of games were rated Everyone (E)
- 30.5 percent of games were rated Teen (T)
- 11.9 percent of games were rated Mature (M)

For more information on the rating system, visit http://www.esrb.com.

Source: Entertainment Software Association

design methods, such as sketching, and/or computer software programs, such as Adobe Illustrator or Macromedia Freehand. The packaging design ideas are then usually presented to the product manager or before a committee for feedback. Prototypes may be developed and analyzed. When a packaging design is agreed upon, the package designer develops the final design layout, and works with the rest of the team until the packaging is produced, handling any last-minute design issues that might occur.

Travisano's own personal favorite design job was for the video game *DDRMAX2: Dance Dance Revolution*, a package he designed mostly from scratch. "The logo was supplied by other artists, but I created the silhouette, the light rays, the vibrant orange background, etcetera, myself. And I'm very pleased with the results. I'm also happy at how popular the game became, which means that many people got to see my work . . . that's pretty satisfying."

REQUIREMENTS

High School
In high school, you should take classes in art and computers, including computer-aided design and graphics, if available. Technical classes such as electrical shop, machine shop, and mechanical drawing will also be helpful when working in the manufacturing industry. In addition to developing artistic abilities, you should also develop communication skills through English and writing classes. Foreign language skills are also beneficial.

Postsecondary Training
Educational requirements vary, but because competition in this field can be fierce, postsecondary education is highly recommended. Some design occupations require a bachelor's degree or a degree from a design school. There are two- and three-year design schools that award certificates or associate's degrees upon completion. Another option is to attend an appropriate college or university to earn a bachelor's or master's degree in fine arts. Programs usually cover core subjects such as English, history, and the sciences, and include various art classes such as design, studio art, and art history. Other beneficial classes include computer-aided design, business administration, basic engineering, computerized design, mechanical drawing, psychology, sales, and marketing.

Other Requirements
If you are interested in packaging design, you should be highly creative, imaginative, have mechanical aptitude and manual dexterity, and verbal and visual communication skills. In addition, you will need

analytical and problem-solving skills and should enjoy working with others because packaging designers often work in teams. You should be familiar with the use of computers in design and manufacturing and be able to work well under pressure. You should also be familiar with computer and video game products. Philip Travisano points out that you will also need a good portfolio of your design work, and a good resume that represents you as "a good worker and reliable person."

EXPLORING

To get a taste of what packaging designing is like, talk to your high school guidance counselor about arranging an interview with someone in the field. Think of some questions you might like to ask, such as how they prepared for the field, what got them interested in the work, and what they like best about their job. Chances are, their answers will be very enlightening to your own search.

While in high school, take as many art classes as you can and get involved in outside projects to further develop your skills. See if you can get some design experience through the theater department, designing costumes, stage sets, or even playbills. Getting involved in the arts is not only fun, but can help you gain a sense of whether or not you enjoy design work.

You can also design packaging for an existing game, or make up a game in need of packaging design. For guidance, look through your own video game collection and pay attention to the elements on the packages that grab your attention. Visit a computer game store and note what games "jump" off the shelf at you, and why. Which packaging details catch your eye? Although you may not have a real game to sell, this exercise will give you an idea of the factors packaging designers in the computer and video game industry face when they set out to design effective packaging.

EMPLOYERS

Packaging designers in the computer and video game industry usually work for manufacturers of the various computer and video game platforms, computer and video game publishers, game development studios, or for a company that offers package design services. Major entertainment software publishers include Electronic Arts, Nintendo of America, Activision, Atari, Sony, Vivendi Universal, THQ, Take 2 Interactive, Microsoft, and Konami Digital Entertainment-America. In addition, designers may be self-employed and work as freelance designers. Opportunities are best in cities and suburbs where business and industry are active, although companies in the computer and video game industry tend to be located in major cities, especially on the East and West Coasts.

Outside of the computer and video game industry, opportunities in the packaging field can be found in almost any company that produces and packages a product. Practically all products, such as food, chemicals, cosmetics, electronics, pharmaceuticals, automotive parts, hardware, and plastics, need to be packaged before reaching the consumer market. Because of this diverse industry, jobs are not restricted to any geographic location or plant size. Philip Travisano noted that before he was in his current position as a video game package designer at Konami, he did design work for toy packages and junk mail and designed company logos as well.

STARTING OUT

Students in a graphic arts program may be able to get job leads through their schools' job placement services. Many jobs in packaging are unadvertised and are discovered through contacts with professionals in the industry. Students may learn about openings from teachers, school administrators, and industry contacts they have acquired during training. Once you learn of a job opening, you will need to have your portfolio ready. Most potential employers require that applicants have a portfolio, or examples of their work, so they can see evidence of an applicant's artistic skills and eye for design.

When it comes to starting out as a packaging designer in the computer and video game industry, Philip Travisano has this to say: "First you've got to have a few nice designs under your belt—whether they are actual jobs that you did for pay, or just good design pieces that you've done for your own portfolio—and then you pretty much have to be in the right place at the right time." Travisano was lucky enough to have found his current position at Konami through an ad he saw on a website, but notes ". . . the best jobs I've ever gotten were by word of mouth; a friend or former colleague heard of a job opening and recommended me." It pays to network: making new contacts and maintaining relationships with previous contacts are invaluable methods for finding out about employment opportunities.

ADVANCEMENT

Packaging designers usually begin in entry-level positions and work their way up as they gain design experience and build their portfolio.

Packaging designers may then advance within the department to become product manager, or they may choose to move into corporate communications and marketing areas. Some designers may choose to be self-employed once they have become well known and gained recognition for quality design work.

Some packaging designers pursue additional education to qualify as design engineers. Others may pursue business, economics, and finance degrees and use these additional skills in other areas of the manufacturing or design industries.

EARNINGS

Earnings for packaging designers vary with the skill level of the employee, the size of the company, and the type of industry. The U.S. Department of Labor reports that the median salary for graphic artists, which includes packaging designers, was $36,630 a year in 2003. The lowest paid 10 percent earned $21,600, while the highest paid 10 percent earned $65,060 or more. A designer who has established an excellent reputation can earn considerably more.

Benefits vary and depend upon the company, but generally include paid holidays, vacations, sick days, and medical and dental insurance. Some companies also offer tuition assistance programs, pension plans, profit sharing, and 401(k) plans. Designers who are freelancers have to provide their own insurance and savings plans.

WORK ENVIRONMENT

Computer and video game packaging designers who work in a manufacturing setting usually work in a studio or office that is well lit and ventilated. However, they may be subjected to odors from glues, paint, and ink when paste-up procedures are used. Also, as computers are used more and more, designers are often sitting in front of a computer for a considerable amount of time.

Occasionally, they may have to be in the noisy factory floor environment when observing product packaging and production. Most plants are clean and well ventilated although actual conditions vary based on the type of product manufactured and packaged. Certain types of industries and manufacturing methods can pose special problems. For example, plants involved in paperboard and paper manufacturing may be very dusty from the use of paper fibers. Plants where electronic components are manufactured may require special conditions to ensure that the environment is free from dirt, contamination, and static. Though these conditions may require some adjustment, in general, most plants have no unusual hazards.

Most computer and video game packaging designers work 40 hours a week, although overtime may be required for the introduction of a new product line or during other busy manufacturing periods.

OUTLOOK

According to the *Occupational Outlook Handbook,* employment of all designers is predicted to grow faster than the average for all occupations through 2012. Opportunities will be good for packaging designers employed in the computer and video game industry and other settings as these businesses will always need talented workers to develop appealing packaging design concepts. However, there is tough competition for the jobs available. Individuals who have little or no formal education and limited experience may find it difficult to find a job.

FOR MORE INFORMATION

For information on graphic design careers, contact
American Institute of Graphic Arts
164 Fifth Avenue
New York, NY 10010
Tel: 212-807-1990
http://www.aiga.org

For computer and video game industry information, contact
Entertainment Software Association
1211 Connecticut Avenue, NW, #600
Washington, DC 20036
Email: esa@theesa.com
http://www.theesa.com

Gamasutra
600 Harrison Street
3rd Floor
San Francisco, CA 94107
Tel: 415-947-6206
http://www.gamasutra.com

For information on careers in industrial design, contact
Industrial Designers Society of America
45195 Business Court, Suite 250
Dulles, VA 20166-6717
Tel: 703-707-6000
Email: idsa@idsa.org
http://www.idsa.org

For information on educational programs, contact
National Association of Schools of Art and Design
11250 Roger Bacon Drive, Suite 21
Reston, VA 20190-5248
Tel: 703-437-0700
Email: info@arts-accredit.org
http://nasad.arts-accredit.org

Producers

OVERVIEW

Producers are the liaison between the creative side of video game development and the business side of marketing and selling the final product. They oversee all steps and processes needed in the creation of a video game, including the hiring, training, and management of staff, checking to see that progress is proceeding according to plan, making sure the project stays within its budget, and finally, shopping around the final product to potential game distributors.

HISTORY

Much has happened in the gaming industry since Atari introduced *Pong* in the early 1970s. Since then, new consoles have come out, including some forgotten hits, such as Intellivision and Colecovision; to more recent names, such as Nintendo, Sega, Sony Play-Station, and Microsoft Xbox. The industry has become a billion-dollar venture, with much to win in the case of a hot game (think *Super Mario Brothers* in its heyday), but also much to lose in the case of a financial sinker (think *E.T. the Extra Terrestrial*—a game so unpopular it actually ended the life of the Atari 2600 console). Because of this financial risk, the job of producer was born, to oversee the creative people working away on the details of the game, while making sure the client and consumer interest would ensure a project was financially viable from the start and would be marketable in the future.

QUICK FACTS

School Subjects
Art
Business
Computer science

Personal Skills
Communication/ideas
Leadership/management

Work Environment
Primarily indoors
Primarily one location

Minimum Education Level
Bachelor's degree

Salary Range
$35,000 to $60,000 to $100,000+

Certification or Licensing
None available

Outlook
Faster than the average

DOT
N/A

GOE
N/A

NOC
N/A

O*NET-SOC
N/A

THE JOB

Producers are responsible for overseeing and managing the development of video and computer games. While they do not generally handle the technical aspects of projects, they are responsible for coordination, management, and overall quality of the final product. At some companies, however, the producer will take on more technical duties, including serving as the lead designer. Most often, the producer is the liaison or "middle man" between the publisher and the game-development team.

Producers must have widely varied knowledge of all aspects of the computer and video game industry. Whether their background is in computers, business, or art, producers must efficiently manage all steps of the development process. They assist the game development staff in the licensing of software, artwork, sound, and other intellectual properties.

Producers have many administrative duties, including scheduling meetings and managing documentation. They are also responsible for general business management duties, including hiring and firing of staff. It is essential that producers are excellent communicators, as they work with and manage all different types of personalities. There are two very different sides to the video game industry—the business side and the creative side. Both executive, financial-minded professionals and creative, art-minded professionals must communicate their ideas to the producer, who is then responsible for collaborating these ideas effectively.

The highest-level producing job is that of the *executive producer,* or *senior producer.* This individual trains, mentors, and manages other producers. The executive producer resolves project conflicts, and may have extended contact with clients. In addition to overseeing all other producers and workers on a project, the executive producer is responsible for obtaining funding, updating clients on the progress of projects, and eventually, finally submitting the final work to the client for approval.

Directly under the executive producer are *lead producers.* These professionals have nontechnical duties, but still work closely with the development team. Lead producers oversee tasks including voiceovers, music, effects, and casting.

Associate producers' main responsibilities are overseeing research and product testing. They hunt and gather information for the development team, as well as oversee video game testers. Associate producers also do more "busy work" such as making client deliveries and taking meeting notes. This may be an entry-level position. Associate producers may have authority over testers, but usually not over any other employees.

Assistant producers, which are also known as *production assistants,* serve as aides to higher-level producers. This occupation is a step toward becoming a producer, but assistants do not usually have much, if any, decision-making authority.

REQUIREMENTS

High School

While an interest in playing video games is obviously a requirement, as a producer you will need to know a lot more about the technical side of game development and testing. For this reason, make sure you create a good foundation by taking math and computer science classes while in high school. Art classes are also useful to stimulate and develop your creative sensibilities, such as illustration—both by hand and with computer drawing tools.

Postsecondary Training

Most larger game developers will require not only its producers, but also its programmers, testers, and other entry-level positions to have a college degree. Bachelor's degrees in computer science with an emphasis in programming or Web design are preferred, though many enter the industry with business degrees that can come in handy when dealing with clients, balancing the budget, and developing a strong business plan.

Other Requirements

While degrees can help get you in the door of the larger companies, experience is what really counts in the gaming industry. If you are a high school graduate with years under your belt as a game tester, programmer, or production assistant, you might just get the job over a recent college graduate with no industry experience.

Because the job of producer includes much administrative work, producers should have working knowledge of basic commercial software, such as Microsoft Office programs and FileMaker Pro. Familiarity with industry software used in game development is also often a requirement, since producers are heavily in the mix of designers, programmers, and testers.

Higher-level producers such as executive producers will need many years of experience managing teams of workers. Communication and mediating skills is a must in this job, since producers are often forced to solve problems among staff members and make decisions

Producers and senior management at a game company view the day's animation work. *(Jim Whitmer Photography)*

based on varying opinions and priorities, such as those of the developer and those of the client.

EXPLORING

To explore this career, make sure to cultivate your love of video games and technology in general. To be able to manage game workers, sell an idea to a client, and make sure all parties are happy while the game is in the works, you had better love the product. But to cultivate this interest in video games doesn't necessarily mean you have to become a hermit with your PlayStation. Many schools and communities host computer science clubs that have special chapters catering to avid gamers. If you can't find such a club, start one with your friends. Schedule tournaments, discuss the best and worst games you've discovered, and think about what makes a game fly off the shelves. This is what a producer has to worry about every day at the office, while still maintaining a passion for playing.

To learn more about the industry and its employers, visit the website of E3, the Electronic Entertainment Expo (http://www.e3expo.com), an annual trade show composed of computer and video game manufacturers from around the world. While the show is closed to the public, the site will give you an idea of what companies are out there.

EMPLOYERS

Producers work for game developers of all sizes. While the largest companies are located on the East and West Coasts and in Texas, Illinois, Maryland, and Massachusetts, smaller employers can be found almost anywhere in the country.

STARTING OUT

Because work experience is valued so highly in this industry, your best bet for landing your first job is with a small, start-up developer. These companies may be more willing to hire less experienced workers in the hopes that they will stay on staff longer than an experienced (and more sought after) producer.

Jobs are easy to find online; most employers post job openings on their company websites or with large job search engines. However, because of the industry's popularity, many open positions do not remain open for long. Jobs often are filled internally or through connections before there ever is a need to post a job classified.

ADVANCEMENT

The jobs of assistant producer or associate producer are entry-level positions, especially if one has worked previously as a game tester or programmer. Advancement comes in the form of higher-level producing jobs—the top position being that of the executive producer, who is responsible for the entire project, beginning to end.

EARNINGS

Associate producers can earn a starting salary of approximately $35,000 to $40,000 a year. Lead producers can earn from $60,000 to $75,000 a year. Executive producers have the highest earning potential, with salaries of $100,000 or more. Earnings vary based on skill, experience, and ability to produce high-quality, top-selling games on time and within budget.

WORK ENVIRONMENT

Producers work in bustling, hectic environments that may be viewed as exciting to some, but stressful to others. To succeed at this job, producers need to be able to juggle many tasks at once and work with varying personalities, from game developers and testers who want to make the game as innovative as possible, to the client whose only interest may be the bottom line. Balancing these (often opposing) priorities can make for a trying, but also exciting, work environment.

OUTLOOK

According to a 2004 survey conducted by the Entertainment Software Association, 53 percent of game players interviewed predicted that in 10 years they would play video games as much or even more than they do now. This increasing demand for challenging and entertaining games creates a steady job market for computer and video game producers. Overall, employment in this job should grow at a faster than average rate through the coming decade.

One caveat: This is a very popular industry. Talented, artistic, business-minded individuals will be drawn to the business of making and selling computer and video games, causing an influx of applicants for limited numbers of jobs. Individuals with more experience will find it the easiest to find jobs. However, with the industry's growth, individuals who are hard working, flexible, and passionate about gaming should be able to find entry-level jobs in computer and video game production.

FOR MORE INFORMATION

IGDA offers professional and academic advice, including information on scholarships. Be sure to check out Breaking In: Preparing for Your Career in Games, *an online guide covering different careers in the visual arts and interviews with top workers in the field.*
International Game Developers Association (IGDA)
600 Harrison Street, 6th Floor
San Francisco, CA 94107
Tel: 415-947-6235
Email: info@igda.org
http://www.igda.org

This trade show features some of the largest and best-known gaming manufacturers in the world. Visit its website for information and links to exhibitors.
Electronic Entertainment Expo (E3)
http://www.e3expo.com

This magazine offers articles on the latest games and top designers and publishes an annual Career Guide *offering tips on breaking into the profession, recommended schools, and more.*
Game Developer
http://www.gdmag.com

Gamejobs.com offers a list of video game companies and available jobs. (You don't have to register or pay to look at job postings.)
GameJobs
http://www.gamejobs.com

Check out this site for articles about job searching and industry developments.
Get in the Game
http://www.gignews.com

INTERVIEW

James Thrush founded Super X Studios (http://www.superxstudios.com) in 1996 and wears many hats at his company, including that of producer/development lead. He has worked in the game development industry for 11 years. Mr. Thrush spoke with the editors of Careers in Focus: Computer & Video Dame Design *about his career.*

Q. What role does a producer/development lead play in the creation of a game?

A. All game projects have either a producer or project manager (or both), whose job it is to manage the project at either a business level (schedules, budget, team building, etc.) and/or a creative level (ensuring creative vision, staffing the creative team). A development lead or lead programmer is the head programmer on the project. They are responsible for managing all the programmers and developing the technical architecture for the project.

Q. Please describe your primary and secondary job duties.

A. Since I run a small company, I have too many duties to list, but they can be separated into primarily: (1) business management (paperwork, marketing, contract negotiations, etc.), (2) project management (hiring team, managing schedule and budget, etc.), and (3) project development (actually building games).

Q. How long does it take to create a typical game?

A. Two to three years for a full-fledged retail game, six to nine months for a smaller, downloadable game.

Q. How did you train for this job?

A. I earned a B.S. in computer engineering. I've studied programming since I was a wee lad, though.

Q. What was your first job in this field? What did you do?

A. I was an intern at Microsoft during college. I was a programmer on multimedia products. Internships are the best. I highly recommend them for all college students.

Q. What are the most important personal and professional qualities for producers?

A. Organizational skills and personal skills.

Q. What are some of the pros and cons of your job?

A. Since I run my own business, I have total personal, professional, and creative freedom to do the kind of work I want, when I want, how I want.

  The down side is working solo for long periods of time when I can't afford to have other people hired on.

Q. What advice would you give young people who are interested in becoming producers?

A. The game development industry, especially producer/management jobs, are especially hard to get into, as there are not that many positions in the entire country and they are highly sought after by many people with years of experience. I would recommend to anyone starting out in the game industry to spend some time researching different positions and figuring out a way to get in the door and get experience. Also, doing personal projects or a portfolio is a great way to showcase your talent for any position (art, programming, producing, etc.).

Q. What's your next big project at Super X Studios?

A. We are currently working on a few products in the Wild Earth brand. There are plenty of ideas in store for future games!

Software Engineers

OVERVIEW

Software engineers are responsible for creating or customizing existing software programs to meet the needs of the computer and video game industry. First, they spend considerable time researching, defining, and analyzing the problem at hand. Then, they develop software programs to resolve the problem on the computer. There are approximately 675,000 computer software engineers employed in many industries in the United States.

HISTORY

The first major advances in modern computer technology were made during World War II. After the war, it was thought that the enormous size of computers, which easily took up the space of entire warehouses, would limit their use to huge government projects. Accordingly, the 1950 census was computer-processed.

The introduction of semiconductors to computer technology made possible smaller and less expensive computers. Businesses began adapting computers to their operations as early as 1954. In the 1960s and beyond, technical societies, trade magazines, and computer organizations sprung up around the country as computer use became more widespread. Within 30 years, computers had revolutionized the way people work, play, and go shopping. Today, computers are everywhere, from businesses of all kinds, to government agencies, charitable organizations, and private homes. Over the years, technology has continued to shrink computer size and increase speed at an unprecedented rate.

QUICK FACTS

School Subjects
Computer science
Mathematics

Personal Skills
Mechanical/manipulative
Technical/scientific

Work Environment
Primarily indoors
Primarily one location

Minimum Education Level
Bachelor's degree

Salary Range
$45,970 to $72,530 to $125,000+

Certification or Licensing
Recommended

Outlook
Much faster than the average

DOT
030

GOE
11.01.01

NOC
2173

O*NET-SOC
15-1031.00, 15-1032.00

Advances in computer technology have enabled professionals to put computers to work in a range of activities once thought impossible. In the past several years, computer software engineers have been able to take advantage of computer hardware improvements in speed, memory capacity, reliability, and accuracy to create programs that do just about anything. Computer engineering blossomed as a distinct subfield in the computer industry after the new performance levels were achieved. This relative lateness is explained by the fact that the programs written by software engineers to solve business and scientific problems are very intricate and complex, requiring a lot of computing power. The computer and video game industry, like many other industries, has taken advantage of the advances in computer technology.

Although many computer scientists will continue to focus their research on further developing hardware, the emphasis in the field has moved more squarely to software, and it is predicted that software engineers will be one of the fastest growing occupations in the United States through the next decade. Given this, software engineering will be an important field in the computer and video game industry for years to come.

THE JOB

Computer software engineers define and analyze specific problems and help develop computer software applications that effectively solve them. Software engineers fall into two basic categories: systems software engineers, who build and maintain entire computer systems for a company; and applications software engineers, who design, create, and modify general computer applications software or specialized utility programs. Additionally, within the computer and video game industry, software engineers can either work on the computer systems and software applications of a computer and video game company, such as a game development studio, computer and video game publisher, or manufacturer of a computer and video game platforms; or they can work directly on computer and video game product development—for example, writing code for a video game or assisting in the programming of a video game console.

Systems software engineers who work on computer systems research how a company's departments and their respective computer systems are organized. They suggest ways to coordinate all these parts. They might set up intranets or networks that link computers within the organization and ease communication.

Some applications software engineers develop packaged software applications, such as word processing, graphic design, or database programs, for software development companies. Other applications software engineers design customized software for individual businesses or organizations. For example, an applications software engineer might work with a video console manufacturer to develop new ways to reduce paperwork in the areas of sales and orders, returns, and bill processing. Applications software engineers write programs using programming languages like C++ and Java.

Software engineering technicians sometimes assist software engineers in completing projects. They are usually knowledgeable in analog, digital, and microprocessor electronics and programming techniques. Technicians know enough about program design and computer languages to fill in details left out by engineers, who conceive of the program from a large-scale perspective. Technicians might also test new software applications with special diagnostic equipment.

Both systems and applications software engineering involve extremely detail-oriented work. Since computers do only what they are programmed to do, engineers have to account for every bit of information with a programming command. Software engineers are thus required to be very well organized and precise. In order to achieve this, they generally follow strict procedures in completing an assignment.

First, they interview clients and colleagues in order to determine exactly what they want the final program to accomplish. Defining the problem by outlining the goal can sometimes be difficult. Then, engineers evaluate the software applications already in use by the client to understand how and why they are failing to fulfill the needs of the operation. After this period of fact gathering, the engineers use methods of scientific analysis and mathematical models to develop possible solutions to the problems. These analytical methods help them predict and measure the outcomes of different proposed designs.

When they have developed a clear idea of what type of program is required to fulfill the client's needs, they draw up a detailed proposal that includes estimates of time and cost allocations. Management must then decide if the project will meet their needs, is a good investment, and whether or not it will be undertaken.

Once a proposal is accepted, both software engineers and technicians begin work on the project. They verify with hardware engineers that the proposed software program can be completed with existing hardware systems. Typically, the engineer writes program specifications and the technician uses his or her knowledge of computer languages to write preliminary programming. Engineers focus most of their effort on program strategies, testing procedures, and reviewing technicians' work.

Software engineers are usually responsible for a significant amount of technical writing, including project proposals, progress reports, and user manuals. They are required to meet regularly with clients in order to keep project goals clear and learn about any changes as quickly as possible.

When the program is completed, the software engineer organizes a demonstration of the final product to the client. Supervisors, management, and users are generally present. Some software engineers may offer to install the program, train users on it, and make arrangements for ongoing technical support.

Software engineers working directly with computer and video games often have very similar job duties to those of a computer programmer working directly with computer and video games. However, there are some differences between the two positions. Software engineers have formal training in methods of scientific analysis. In general, programmers are concerned with writing code for a game, whereas engineers are concerned with not just writing the code, but how that code relates to the game application in which it will be used, or how that code figures in the "big picture" in terms of what is to be accomplished. Software engineers can be game programmers, but not all game programmers have the skills to be software engineers. Regardless, in many computer and video game companies there is a lot of overlap between the two positions and the terms are often used interchangeably. That said, for more specific information about the job duties of a software engineer working directly with computer and video games, see the "Computer Programmers" article in this book.

REQUIREMENTS
High School
If you are interested in pursuing this career, take as many computer, math, and science courses as possible, because they provide fundamental math and computer knowledge and teach analytical thinking skills. Classes that rely on schematic drawing and flowcharts are also very valuable. English and speech courses will help you improve your communication skills, which are very important for software engineers.

Postsecondary Training
In the past, the computer industry has tended to be fairly flexible about official credentials; demonstrated computer proficiency and work experience have often been enough to obtain a good position. As more and more well-educated professionals enter the industry,

Top 10 Entertainment Software Publishers in the United States

Company	Website	Market Share
1. Electronic Arts	http://www.ea.com	16.5 percent
2. Nintendo of America	http://www.nintendo.com	11.6 percent
3. Activision	http://www.activision.com	7.1 percent
4. Atari (formerly Infogrames)	http://www.infogrames.com	6.1 percent
5. Sony	http://www.us.playstation.com	6.1 percent
6. Vivendi Universal	http://www.vugames.com	5.7 percent
7. THQ	http://www.thq.com	4.9 percent
8. Take 2 Interactive	http://www.take2games.com	4.1 percent
9. Microsoft	http://www.xbox.com	3.6 percent
10. Konami of America	http://www.konami.com/usa	2.9 percent

Source: Wedbursh Morgan Securities, May 2002 Report

however, it is becoming more important for you to have at least a bachelor's degree in computer science, software engineering, or programming.

Certification or Licensing

Another option is to pursue commercial certification. These programs are usually run by computer companies that wish to train professionals to work with their products. Classes are challenging and examinations can be rigorous. New programs are introduced every year. In addition, professional certification as a certified software development professional is now offered by the Institute of Electrical and Electronics Engineers (IEEE) Computer Society. The Institute for Certification of Computing Professionals also offers general certifications to computer professionals.

Other Requirements

As a software engineer, you will need strong communication skills in order to be able to make formal business presentations and interact with people having different levels of computer expertise. You must also be detail oriented. Working with programming languages and intense details is often frustrating. Therefore, you should be patient, enjoy problem-solving challenges, and work well under pressure.

EXPLORING

In general, you should be intent on learning as much as possible about computers and computer software. You should learn about new developments by reading trade magazines and talking to other computer users. You also can join computer clubs and surf the Internet for information about working in this field. Visit the website of the International Game Developers Association (http://www.igda.org/breakingin) to check out *Breaking In: Preparing for Your Career in Games*. This free online publication offers an overview of the different jobs-including engineers—available in the game industry and features job profiles and interviews of workers in the field. Familiarizing yourself with the many different types of computer and video games is also a great way to become familiar with the various products of the industry.

Try to spend a day with a working software engineer or technician in order to experience firsthand what their job is like. School guidance counselors can help you arrange such a visit. You can also talk to your high school computer teacher for more information.

High school and college students who can operate a computer may be able to obtain part-time jobs or internships at companies that produce computer and video games. Any computer experience will be helpful for future computer training.

EMPLOYERS

Approximately 675,000 computer software engineers are employed in many areas of business in the United States. Approximately 394,000 work with applications and 281,000 work with systems software. In the computer and video game industry, most software engineers are employed by the manufacturers of the various computer and video game platforms, computer and video game publishers, and game development studios. These companies are usually located in major cities, especially on the East and West Coasts. A significant number of game companies are also located in Illinois and Texas. Major entertainment software publishers include Electronic Arts, Nintendo of America, Activision, Atari, Sony, Vivendi Universal, THQ, Take 2 Interactive, Microsoft, and Konami of America.

Outside of the computer and video game industry, software engineering is done in many fields, including medical, industrial, military, communications, aerospace, scientific, and other commercial businesses. The majority of software engineers, though, are employed by computer and data processing companies and by consulting firms.

STARTING OUT

As a college student, you should work closely with your schools' career services offices, as many professionals find their first position through on-campus recruiting. Career services office staff are well trained to provide tips on resume writing, interviewing techniques, and locating job leads.

Individuals not working with a school placement office can check the classified ads for job openings. Software engineers who are specifically interested in working in the game industry can visit the websites of computer and video game companies and developers and sites that advertise job openings, such as Game Jobs (http://www.gamejobs.com) and Gamasutra (http://www.gamasutra.com).

Some software engineers interested in the game industry attend trade shows (such as the annual Computer Game Developers Conference) where they can meet recruiters looking for people to work at their companies. Information on the conference is available at http://www.gdconf.com.

ADVANCEMENT

Software engineers who demonstrate leadership qualities and thorough technical know-how may become *project team leaders* who are responsible for full-scale game software development projects. Project team leaders oversee the work of technicians and other engineers. They determine the overall parameters of a project, calculate time schedules and financial budgets, divide the project into smaller tasks, and assign these tasks to engineers. Overall, they do both managerial and technical work.

Software engineers with experience as project team leaders may be promoted to a position as *software manager,* running a large research and development department. Managers oversee software projects with a more encompassing perspective; they help choose projects to be undertaken, select project team leaders and engineering teams, and assign individual projects. In some cases, they may be required to travel, solicit new business, and contribute to the general marketing strategy of the company.

Many computer professionals find that their interests change over time. As long as individuals are well qualified and keep up to date with the latest technology, they are usually able to find positions in other areas of the computer industry.

EARNINGS

Computer software engineers with a bachelor's degree in computer engineering earned starting salaries of $51,343 in 2003, according to the National Association of Colleges and Employers. New computer engineers with a master's degree averaged $64,200. Computer engineers specializing in applications earned median annual salaries of $72,530 in 2003, according to the U.S. Department of Labor. The lowest 10 percent averaged less than $45,970; the highest 10 percent earned $111,860 or more annually. Software engineers specializing in systems software earned median salaries of $76,240 in 2003. The lowest paid 10 percent averaged less than $47,870 annually, and the highest paid engineers made more than $114,070 per year. Experienced software engineers can earn more than $125,000 a year. When software engineers are promoted to project team leader or software manager, they earn even more. Software engineers generally earn more in geographical areas where there are clusters of computer companies, such as the Silicon Valley in northern California.

Most software engineers work for companies that offer extensive benefits, including health insurance, sick leave, and paid vacation. In some smaller game companies, however, benefits may be limited.

WORK ENVIRONMENT

Software engineers usually work in comfortable office environments. Overall, they usually work 40-hour weeks, but this depends on the nature of the employer and expertise of the engineer. In the computer and video game industry, long work hours are typical. In consulting firms, for example, it is typical for engineers to work long hours and frequently travel to out-of-town assignments.

Software engineers generally receive an assignment and a time frame within which to accomplish it; daily work details are often left up to the individuals. Some engineers work relatively lightly at the beginning of a project, but work a lot of overtime at the end in order to catch up. Most engineers are not compensated for overtime. Software engineering can be stressful, especially when engineers must work to meet deadlines.

OUTLOOK

The field of software engineering is expected to be one of the fastest growing occupations through 2012, according to the U.S. Department of Labor. Demands made on computers increase every day and from all industries, including the computer and video game industry. The development of one kind of software sparks ideas for many others. In addition, users rely on software programs that are increasingly user-friendly.

Since technology changes so rapidly, software engineers are advised to keep up on the latest developments. While the need for software engineers will remain high, computer languages will probably change every few years and software engineers will need to attend seminars and workshops to learn new computer languages and software design. They also should read trade magazines (especially those that relate to the game industry), surf the Internet, and talk with colleagues about the field. These kinds of continuing education techniques help ensure that software engineers are best equipped to meet the needs of the workplace.

FOR MORE INFORMATION

For information on internships, student membership, and the student magazine Crossroads, *contact*
Association for Computing Machinery
1515 Broadway
New York, NY 10036
Tel: 800-342-6626
Email: sigs@acm.org
http://www.acm.org

For information on careers in the game industry, contact
International Game Developers Association
600 Harrison Street, 6th Floor
San Francisco, CA 94107
Phone: 415-947-6235
Email: info@igda.org
http://www.igda.org

For computer and video game industry information, contact
Entertainment Software Association
1211 Connecticut Avenue, NW, #600
Washington, DC 20036
Email: esa@theesa.com
http://www.theesa.com

Gamasutra
600 Harrison Street, 3rd Floor
San Francisco, CA 94107
Tel: 415-947-6206
http://www.gamasutra.com

For certification information, contact
Institute for Certification of Computing Professionals
2350 East Devon Avenue, Suite 115
Des Plaines, IL 60018-4610
Tel: 800-843-8227
http://www.iccp.orgs

*For information on certification, scholarships, student membership,
and the student newsletter* looking.forward, *contact*
IEEE Computer Society
1730 Massachusetts Avenue, NW
Washington, DC 20036-1992
Tel: 202-371-0101
Email: membership@computer.org
http://www.computer.org

For more information on careers in computer software, contact
Software and Information Industry Association
1090 Vermont Ave, NW, Sixth Floor
Washington, DC 20005
Tel: 202-289-7442
http://www.siia.net

INTERVIEW

*Steve Coallier is a development director at Electronic Arts (EA), one
of the largest game companies in the industry. He has worked in the
computer and video game industry for nearly 15 years. Steve spoke
with the editors of* Careers in Focus: Computer & Video Game
Design *about his career and what the future holds for EA.*

Q. What are your duties as a development director?

A. My primary duty is making sure that the game I am working on
is developed on time, on or under budget, and with the highest
degree of quality and completeness possible given the project's
allotted schedule and resources. My secondary duties are to
make sure that the people in my reporting structure are getting

everything they need in order to make that happen, and also to make sure that their careers grow and advance as they continue to do good work for Electronic Arts. The job is different every single day.

During a game project, all of the artists and engineers report to me, and in turn, I report to the project's executive producer. As games grow in size in scope, sometimes a team will have multiple development directors reporting to a senior development director. Our current project is large enough to warrant this, so I report to a senior development director.

Q. How did you get into this career?

A. The way I got in is now rare—I answered a classified ad from the *Fresno Bee* looking for game testers. I was a tester for about six months, and then begged to do something else. Playing games for money sounds like a lot of fun, but you have to remember three things. First, the games you play aren't necessarily games you like to play. Second, the whole time you're playing them, they're broken, because it's your job to find all the problems with them. And lastly, as soon as they're not broken any more, you move on to something else that is! So, at that point, I had the opportunity to be either an artist or an engineer, and I chose engineer because there was (I thought) a lot more challenge and variety in the work. I have been very happy with my choice.

Q. With the understanding that there are many types of games, what are the basic qualities that make up any good game?

A. One of the old EA adages for this is that games should be "Simple, Hot, and Deep." By simple, we mean easy to learn how to play. This is more true nowadays than it ever was, with games reaching a wider and wider audience that includes a lot more "casual" gamers than the industry catered to for a long time. The term hot means the game should be fun and exciting. Finally, deep means the game should be feature rich—whether it's a complex and engaging world or a more simple game that has different game modes to choose from.

In my own terms, I think that a game should draw the player forward—the games that somehow encourage the player to play for just a little while longer seem to be the most successful. Generally this is done through what we call scoring and rewards—if you play for just a little while longer, you will reach the next fun and cool reward! This is actually a principle that's been around since the early days of coin-op games where man-ufacturers were trying to squeeze more quarters out of players' pockets, but it still applies today.

Q. What is your favorite game that you have worked on and why?

A. This is certainly a tough call. I've worked on a lot of good games. I would probably choose *Knockout Kings 2000*. It was a lot of fun to work on and I worked with a fantastic team. The game came out great, it came out on time, and it firmly established EA's posi-tion as the leader in boxing simulations.

Q. Electronics Arts is the top, or one of the top, companies in the game business. What type of qualities does it look for in potential employees? What makes your company stand out from the others?

A. EA looks for a strong passion for games, it looks for talent, brains, and quick learners (in any discipline), and it looks for peo-ple who can work well with a team in order to get a project fin-ished. Apart from employing the lion's share of talented game developers within the industry, EA offers the flexibility and resources—both financial and human—to build projects that most other companies couldn't pull off the way we can. I often point to the pre-launch days of the PlayStation 2 as an example of this. We had people in each of our studios working on titles for launch, and they all did an excellent job of operating as a team. They shared problems and collaborated on solutions, and I think this is a huge factor in why our market share on that plat-form was over 40 percent at launch. That kind of development community is just a pleasure to be a part of!

Q. What does the future hold for EA?

A. I expect the future of EA is to branch out into other forms of games and entertainment. The line between movies and games is blurring, and as technology changes, I think EA will become more of a factor in film as we are on consoles and PCs. We are just beginning to take some solid strides in online games as well, and I think that's going to provide a tremendous boost to our growth. I know that whatever the future holds for EA, it's going to be interesting and it's going to be fun!

Q. **I've read that you're very interested in Legos. Can you tell us what type of objects that you've created and how you get into Legoing (is that a word?)**

A. On behalf of The Lego Group, I am almost required to correct you: the plural of Lego is Lego [grin]. I had Lego as a kid in the 70s, of course, but I got away from it for a while and didn't venture back until the mid-90s. I originally got interested because I was thinking of making my cubicle—EA was almost all cubicles at that point—into an office by extending the walls upward with Lego. I found out how ridiculously expensive that would be, but I started to build things anyway. My first two projects were a scale model of a plane that I'd been stunt flying in (again, thanks to EA) and Scott Adams' Dogbert character from the *Dilbert* comic strip. Since then I've done dozens of pieces including a five-and-a-half foot model of the Transamerica Building in San Francisco and a life-sized model of Superman.

Lego is a great hobby for software engineers because often when a project is building, there's not really enough time to do much of anything else. My Superman, for instance, was mostly built five or 10 minutes at a time at work throughout the course of about 18 months while *Knockout Kings* and *NASCAR* were building.

Software Store Employees

OVERVIEW

Software store employees are *retail sales workers* who work in stores that sell computer software and related products, including computer and video games. They assist customers with purchases by identifying their needs, showing or demonstrating merchandise, receiving payment, recording sales, and wrapping their purchases or arranging for their delivery. They are sometimes called sales clerks, retail clerks, or salespeople. There are approximately 4.1 million retail salespersons employed in the United States.

HISTORY

Although stores dedicated entirely to computer and video games are commonplace today, that wasn't always the case. The first computer and video game sold for home use was Magnavox's *Odyssey*. It was released in 1972 and was only available for sale through Magnavox stores. Video consoles, and the games that were played on them, quickly arrived on the market after that, and most were sold through standard department stores, such as Sears; electronic stores, such as Radio Shack; and toy stores.

As general computer and electronics technology progressed, so did the opening of stores focused primarily on entertainment products—music, movies, and computer and video games. Some stores previously providing only music products branched out into stocking computer and video games. Computer stores routinely stocked computer and video games as more and more popular games were produced for PCs and Macs and consumer demand warranted it. General discount retail stores like Wal-Mart and Target also started carrying computer and video game titles.

Stores devoted entirely to computer and video games—GameStop, Babbage's, FuncoLand, and EB Games, for example—have been around for much of the life of the computer and game industry. Some have been around since the 1980s; others are newcomers to the industry.

Today, computer and video games are sold in a wide variety of retail establishments, providing many employment options for software store employees in the computer and video game industry.

THE JOB

Software store employees work in many different types of retail establishments that sell software, and in a variety of roles. Some, for example, work in small specialty shops focusing on computer and video games, where, in addition to waiting on customers, they might check inventory, order stock from sales representatives (or by telephone or mail), place newspaper display advertisements, prepare window displays, and rearrange merchandise for sale.

Other software store employees may work in specific departments, such as the computer department or electronics department of a large store. The employees in a department work in shifts to provide service to customers six or seven days a week. To improve their sales effectiveness and knowledge of merchandise, they may attend regular staff meetings. The primary responsibility of software store employees is to interest customers in the merchandise and answer any questions customers may have so the customer feels comfortable making a purchase. Employees often do this by describing the product's features or demonstrating its use. Many stores have the latest computer or video games and their platforms on display, available so customers can test the products themselves. Employees are on hand to point out the latest advances in the technology and answer any questions. Some workers must have specialized knowledge, particularly those who work in stores that advertise software as their specialty.

In addition to selling, most software store employees make out sales checks; receive cash, check, and charge payments; bag or package purchases; and give change and receipts. Depending on the hours they work, they might have to open or close the cash register. This might include counting the money in the cash register; separating charge slips, coupons, and exchange vouchers; and making deposits

Game Tips

Having trouble playing your favorite game? The following websites will help you slay that pesky dragon, karate-chop your way past hundreds of ninja warriors, or advance to the temple in the clouds to fight the grand master:

Gamesfaqs.com (also features lists of game companies and discussion boards)
http://www.gamefaqs.com

Planetdeusex.com (also includes articles, interviews, and discussion forums)
http://planetdeusex.com

Universal Hint System (also features game reviews)
http://www.uhs-hints.com

at the cash office. The sales records they keep are normally used in inventory control. Employees are often held responsible for the contents of their registers, and repeated shortages are cause for dismissal in many organizations.

Software store employees must be aware of any promotions the store is sponsoring and know the store's policies and procedures, especially on returns and exchanges. Also, they often must recognize possible security risks and know how to handle such situations.

Consumers often form their impressions of a store by its sales force. To stay ahead in the fiercely competitive retail industry, employers are expected to provide courteous and efficient service at all times. When a customer wants a product that is not on the sales floor, for example, the employee might be expected to check the stockroom and, if necessary, place a special order or call another store to locate the item. And, as is often the case with long-awaited software or a new computer or video game, employees might be required to set up a presale or wait list for customers who want to guarantee that they will have the new product as soon as it is released to the public.

REQUIREMENTS

High School
Employers generally prefer to hire high school graduates for most sales positions. Such subjects as English, speech, and mathematics

provide a good background for these jobs. Also, since you will be selling computer software, any computer classes you can take will also be useful. Many high schools and two-year colleges have special programs that include courses in merchandising, principles of retailing, and retail selling.

Postsecondary Training

In retail sales, as in other fields, the level of opportunity tends to coincide with the level of a person's education. In many stores, college graduates enter immediately into on-the-job training programs to prepare them for management assignments. Successful and experienced workers who do not have a degree might also qualify for these programs. Useful college courses include economics, business administration, and marketing. Many colleges offer majors in retailing. Executives in many companies express a strong preference for liberal arts graduates, especially those with some business courses or a master's degree in business administration. Any computer classes you can take will also be useful and help prepare you to better serve customers in the retail software environment.

Other Requirements

Software store employees must be in good health. Many selling positions require standing most of the day. They must have stamina to face the grueling pace of busy times, such as weekends and the Christmas season, while at the same time remaining pleasant and effective. Personal appearance is important. Salespeople should be neat and well groomed and have an outgoing personality.

A pleasant speaking voice, natural friendliness, tact, and patience are all helpful personal characteristics. Software store employees must be able to converse easily with strangers of all ages. In addition to interpersonal skills, sales workers must be equally good with figures. They should be able to add and subtract accurately and quickly and operate cash registers and other types of business machines.

Software store employees should be very familiar with the latest games and technology. Many customers will have questions—for example, asking if a game is compatible with their particular type of computer, or asking for recommendations on games, based on the age and interests of the intended recipient. Salespersons who are knowledgeable about the products they sell are more effective salespersons and more attractive to employers.

Most states have established minimum standards that govern retail employment. Some states set a minimum age of 14, require at least a high school diploma, or prohibit more than eight hours of work a day

Software store employees need to be very familiar with the latest games and technology in order to explain new products to customers. *(Index Stock Imagery)*

or 48 hours in any six days. These requirements are often relaxed for those people employed during the Christmas season.

EXPLORING

Because of its seasonal nature, retailing offers numerous opportunities for temporary or part-time sales experience. Most stores add extra personnel for the Christmas season. Fewer sales positions are available in metropolitan areas during the summer, as this is frequently the slowest time of the year, but vacation areas may hire sales employees—typically high school or college students.

Many high schools and junior colleges have developed "distributive education" programs that combine courses in retailing with part-time work in the field. The distributive education student may receive academic credit for this work experience in addition to regular wages. Software store owners cooperating in these programs often hire students as full-time personnel upon completion of the program.

EMPLOYERS

Retail stores that are devoted entirely to selling computer and video games are the obvious employer of software salespersons.

According to *Video Business* magazine, two retailers, GameStop and EB Games, control approximately 25 percent of the retail computer and video game market. In 2004, GameStop had 1,472 stores (known under the names GameStop, Babbage's, FuncoLand, and Software Etc.) in the United States, and EB Games had 1,436 locations (known under the names EB Games and Electronic Boutique). There are also many other retail environments where games are sold, giving a software salesperson many opportunities to find an employer. Department stores; discount stores; home electronics stores; "entertainment" stores, which sell music, movies, and games; toy stores; and computer stores are just a few examples of retail establishments that sell computer and video games, thus having a need for software salespersons. Some examples of stores that fall under this second category include Best Buy, Blockbuster, Circuit City, CompUSA, Wal-Mart, Toys "R" Us, Barnes & Noble, and Borders.

STARTING OUT

If they have openings, retail stores usually hire beginning salespeople who come in and fill out an application. Major department stores maintain extensive personnel departments, while in smaller stores the manager might do the hiring. Occasionally, sales applicants are given an aptitude test.

An applicant might be hired for sales positions and immediately start working in sales. In some stores, especially larger stores, they might instead begin by working in the stockroom as clerks, helping to set up merchandise displays, or assisting in the receiving or shipping departments. After a while they might be moved up to a sales assignment.

Training varies with the type and size of the store. In large stores, the beginner might benefit from formal training courses that discuss sales techniques, store policies, the mechanics of recording sales, and an overview of the entire store. Programs of this type are usually followed by on-the-job sales supervision. The beginner in a small store might receive personal instruction from the manager or a senior sales worker, followed by supervised sales experience. The level of instruction an employee receives regarding the products sold in the store tends to vary among the many retail stores that sell computer and video games. An employee in a store devoted to computer and video games or computer software is generally expected to be more knowledgeable about computers and games than the average person is. These stores tend to offer more training and instruction regarding the games, system requirements, and platforms sold in the store. An employee in a store where the focus is not on computers and games might not receive comparable training or instruction. Rather, they will likely be expected to work with general merchandise in the store, in several different departments.

College graduates and people with successful sales experience often enter executive training programs (sometimes referred to as flying squads because they move rapidly through different parts of the store). As they rotate through various departments, the trainees are exposed to merchandising methods, stock and inventory control, advertising, buying, credit, and personnel. By spending time in each of these areas, trainees receive a broad retailing background designed to help them as they advance into the ranks of management.

ADVANCEMENT

Large stores or corporations have the most opportunities for promotion. Retailing, however, is a mobile field, and successful and experienced people can readily change employment. This is one of the few fields where advancement to executive positions is possible regardless of education, as long as a software salesperson has the necessary initiative and ability.

When first on the job, software store workers can enhance their career potential by specializing in a particular line of merchandise and cultivating good sales skills. They become authorities on a certain product line or subject area, like the computer and video game industry. Many good retail sales workers prefer the role of the senior sales worker and remain at this level. Others might be asked to become supervisor of a section. Eventually they might develop into a department manager, floor manager, division or branch manager, or general manager. They might become a *district manager*, and supervise several retail stores within a geographical location.

People with retail sales experience often enter related areas, such as buying. Other retail store workers can advance into support areas, such as personnel, accounting, public relations, and credit.

Young people with ability find that retailing offers the opportunity for unusually rapid advancement. One study revealed that half of all retail executives are under 35 years of age. It is not uncommon for a person under 35 to be in charge of a retail store or department with an annual sales volume of over $1 million. Conversely, the retail executive who makes bad merchandising judgments might quickly be out of a job.

EARNINGS

Most beginning software store workers start at the federal minimum wage, which is $5.15 an hour. Wages vary greatly, depending primarily on the type of store and the degree of skill required. Businesses might offer higher wages to attract and retain workers. Some software store workers make as much as $12 an hour or more.

Department stores or retail chains might pay more than smaller stores. Higher wages are paid for positions requiring a greater degree of skill. Many sales workers also receive a commission (often 4 to 8 percent) on their sales or are paid solely on commission. According to the *Occupational Outlook Handbook,* median hourly earnings of retail salespersons, including commission, were $8.51 in 2002. Wages ranged from less than $6.18 to more than $16.96 an hour. Sales workers in department stores earned average hourly salaries of $8.12 in 2002.

Salespeople in many retail stores are allowed a discount on their own purchases, ranging from 10 to 25 percent. This privilege is sometimes extended to the worker's family. Meals in the employee cafeterias maintained by large stores might be served at a price that is below cost. Many stores provide sick leave, medical and life insurance, and retirement benefits for full-time workers. Most stores give paid vacations.

WORK ENVIRONMENT

Software store workers are classified as retail sales workers, and generally work in clean, comfortable, well-lighted areas. Those with seniority have reasonably good job security. When business is slow, stores might curtail hiring and not fill vacancies that occur. Most stores, however, are able to weather mild business recessions without having to lay off experienced employees. During periods of economic recession, competition among retail salespeople for job openings can become intense.

The 9-to-5, Monday-through-Friday schedule is not common in retailing. Most retail salespeople can expect to work some evening and weekend hours, and longer than normal hours might be scheduled during Christmas and other peak periods. In addition, most retailers restrict the use of vacation time between Thanksgiving and early January. Most retail sales workers receive overtime pay during Christmas and other rush seasons. Part-time retail salespeople generally work at peak hours of business, supplementing the full-time staff. Because competition in the retailing business is keen, many retailers work under pressure. Retail sales workers might not be directly involved but will feel the pressures of the industry in subtle ways. They must be able to adjust to alternating periods of high activity and dull monotony. No two days—or even customers—are alike. Because some customers are hostile and rude, salespeople must learn to exercise tact and patience at all times.

OUTLOOK

Software store employees are classified as retail sales workers. The employment of retail sales workers should grow about as fast as the average for all occupations through 2012, according to the U.S. Department of Labor. Because turnover among sales workers is much higher than average, many of the expected employment opportunities will stem from the need to replace workers. Other positions will result from existing stores' staffing for longer business hours or reducing the length of the average employee workweek.

Several factors—the full effects of which have yet to be measured—might reduce the long-range demand for sales personnel. As some stores rapidly convert to self-service operations, they will need fewer sales workers. In contrast, many other stores are trying to stay competitive by offering better customer service and more sales staff attention. For example, some software and electronics stores are adding personal shopping assistants as a way to provide stronger customer service.

At the same time, many products, including computer hardware and software do not lend themselves to self-service operations. These products require extremely skilled employees to assist customers and explain the benefits of various makes and models. On balance, as easy-to-sell goods will be increasingly marketed in self-service stores, the demand in the future will be strongest for retail sales workers who are knowledgeable about particular types of products.

There should continue to be good opportunities for temporary and part-time workers, especially during the holidays. All retail stores are particularly interested in people who, by returning year after year, develop good sales backgrounds.

FOR MORE INFORMATION

For computer and video game industry information, contact
Entertainment Software Association
1211 Connecticut Avenue, NW, #600
Washington, DC 20036
Email: esa@theesa.com
http://www.theesa.com

Gamasutra
600 Harrison Street, 3rd Floor
San Francisco, CA 94107
Tel: 415-947-6206
http://www.gamasutra.com

For industry information, contact
Interactive Entertainment Merchants Association
64 Danbury Road, Suite 700
Wilton, CT 06897-4406
Tel: 203-761-6180
http://www.iema.org

For materials on educational programs in the retail industry, contact
National Retail Federation
325 7th Street, NW, Suite 1100
Washington, DC 20004
Tel: 800-673-4692
http://www.nrf.com

For more information on the retail software industry, visit
Stores
http://www.stores.org

Video Business
http://www.videobusiness.com

Sound Workers

QUICK FACTS

School Subjects
Computer science
Music

Personal Skills
Artistic/creative
Technical/scientific

Work Environment
Primarily indoors
Primarily one location

Minimum Education Level
Some postsecondary training

Salary Range
$45,000 to $57,500 to
$130,000+

Certification or Licensing
None available

Outlook
About as fast as the average

DOT
152, 194

GOE
01.04.04, 01.04.02, 05.10.05

NOC
5132, 5133, 5225

O*NET-SOC
27-4014.00, 27-2041.00,
27-2041.02, 27-2041.03,
27-2042.00, 27-2042.02

OVERVIEW

Computer and video game *sound workers* are responsible for creating the audio aspects of computer and video games. Their work is essential to a game's success—adding to a game's intensity and dimension and enhancing gamers' playing experiences. Ironically, though, when sound workers have done their jobs well, the sound becomes such an integral part of the video game that few players notice it as a separate, painstakingly developed game element. At the start of the video game age, the technologies available limited a game's sound to simple noises, such as a "pong" or a "beep, beep, beep." Since then sound capabilities have developed dramatically so that players can actually hear the game world they've entered through such things as surround sound, characters speaking naturally, noises in the game's environment, and full musical compositions.

HISTORY

At the beginning of the video game age, developers naturally focused on game play and visuals. Today, with ever faster computer processors, increasing storage space, a variety of equipment on which to play—from the Internet to the home console—and sophisticated recording and editing software and hardware, sound workers are gaining in both importance and the respect they receive. Audio is one of the most rapidly developing areas of game work, and many in the industry see this field as one that will have dynamic future growth.

THE JOB

Some sound workers are employed by large, well-known companies, such as Nintendo, on a full-time basis. Many sound workers, however, work on a contract basis, meaning that they are freelancers who are hired by companies to work on a particular project, and sometimes a particular aspect of a particular project, until it is completed. Because of this and other factors, such as the size of the employer, sound workers are referred to by a number of job titles. In addition, they may be responsible for many types of sound production or focus on only a few sound areas.

Sound designers, sometimes known as *sound engineers,* are responsible for all of the sound used in a computer or video game. They create the squealing noise of a race car's tires, the squish of a character walking through mud, the zap from an alien's weapon, or the crunching thud of one football player tackling another. They are also responsible for any talking, singing, yelling, and so on, that characters in the game do. Finally, they create or find recordings of all of the music to be used in the game. All of a game's sounds must fit in with its action and setting in order to draw players in and increase their emotional experience with the game. Sound that doesn't fit will be jarring and can end up annoying players and even ruining the game experience. Therefore, to do their job successfully, sound workers must work well with other game team members to ensure that the sound they create fits just right.

The first team members that sound designers usually consult are the game designers. It is the sound designer's job to find out what look and feel the game designers want. To do this, the sound designer may look at concept sketches and ask the game designers questions. How many levels of play will there be? Who is the intended audience? Where will the game be played (for example, in an arcade, on the Internet, or on a console)? Does the game take place in a particular time period, such as 100 years in the future or during the Civil War? Answers to questions like these give sound designers a framework for their work. For example, if the game will be played in an arcade, the designer will know to make sounds louder and simpler than for a game played on a console at home. If the game takes place in the past, for example, the sound designer may need to do research to find out what musical instruments were used then and then find ways to reproduce their sound.

Sound designers also frequently work with artists and animators. To enhance the game, sound designers must make sure the characters' voices somehow compliment their looks as well as match up with the artists and animators' visions of their personalities. For example, the sound designer needs to know if a large, bear-like character should have a deep, slow-speaking, friendly voice or squeaky, fast-speaking, unpleasant voice. Voices also need to match up with the character's actions. In some sports games, for example, a commentator may speak during much of the game but will need to adjust his or her voice—from fast and excited to disappointed to surprised, and so on—to suit the events. Sound designers also work with game programmers to ensure that the final sound produced is what was desired. Although sound designers generally don't have to write the programming code, those who have coding knowledge are at an advantage because they have a good understanding of both the programmer's job and how to achieve the best sound style.

Sound designers usually have access to a "sound library," recordings of many different sounds. But they must also know how to create and record their own sounds for use in a game. This can mean recording sounds that will be used realistically in the game world; for example, recording the noise of a passing train to use in a game scene with a passing train. It can also mean recording sounds to go with imaginary action in a game; for example, recording a rotten apple hitting a brick wall to use for the game sound of a zombie being punched in the stomach. Sound designers create music using special software and equipment, such as a keyboard that simulates many instruments. They may write the music, play it, and record it (or they may hire composers and musicians to write and perform the music). Occasionally they may make a recording of live music and even be responsible for finding the right musicians for the work. In addition, game designers sometimes ask the sound designer to use music that has already been produced, such as songs from a popular band. For example, *Tony Hawk's Pro Skater 3* incorporates music from well-known punk rock bands such as Motorhead and the Ramones. *Music licensors* are the professionals who negotiate with music labels and up-and-coming bands for the rights to use music in the games. In that case, either the sound designer or a music licensor needs to get permission to use the music from the recording label. Sound designers also record the actors who do the voice-overs for the game characters. Again, sound designers are sometimes responsible for finding actors to do this work, or they may do some of the voice-overs themselves.

The extent of sound designers' responsibilities depends a great deal on factors such as their experience, the size of the employer, and the budget for creating the game. In an environment that offers the opportunity to specialize, such as at a large company, there may be sound designers who work only on sound effects. These *sound effects*

A sound designer edits game audio in his studio. *(Jim Whitmer Photography)*

designers concentrate on creating the noises for specific events in a game—a car crash, a baseball being hit, a bomb exploding, and so on—as well as background noises, such as rain falling or a dog barking far away.

Composers are sound specialists who focus on creating the music for a game. They need to be able to write music in many different styles—techno, rock, and even classical—for different games and to create many different moods. Frequently composers know how to play an instrument on their own, and many find that knowing how to play the piano, synthesizers, or samplers is particularly helpful. *Musicians* perform, compose, conduct, and arrange music for computer and video games. They may work alone or as part of a group to create music. Some composers and musicians may also have additional duties as sound designers or sound effects designers. To create the various types of sound and music that appear in games, composers and musicians may work from storyboards, a finished game, or nothing but an idea or concept for the game.

REQUIREMENTS

High School

If you are interested in becoming a sound worker, you should take computer science and math, including algebra and geometry. You should also take history, English, and other college prep classes. Of course, take as many music classes as possible and learn how to play one or more musical instruments, especially the piano, synthesizer, and keyboard.

Postsecondary Training
In the past, most sound designers learned their trade through on-the-job training. Today, many sound designers are earning bachelor's degrees in music, sound design, or audio engineering, and this will probably become more necessary as technologies become more complex. Typical programs focus on computer and music studies, including music history, music theory, composition, sound design, and audio engineering.

If you are interested in becoming a composer or musician, you can continue your education in any of numerous colleges and universities or special music schools or conservatories that offer bachelor's and higher degrees. Your course of study will include music history, music criticism, music theory, harmony, counterpoint, rhythm, melody, and ear training. In most major music schools, courses in composition are offered along with orchestration and arranging. Courses are also taught covering voice and the major musical instruments, including keyboard, guitar, and, more recently, synthesizer. Most schools now cover computer techniques as applied to music as well.

Other Requirements
Sound designers need to be able to use the latest technologies to record, edit, and "sweeten" their work. Workers in this field are continuously updating their skills, learning how to use new tools or techniques to create the sounds they want. Composers and musicians need to have a passion for music, an interest in computer and video games, and a high degree of dedication, self-discipline, and drive. All sound workers should also have strong communication skills to be able to work with a diverse group of game industry professionals and have flexibility to work with a variety of musical genres.

EXPLORING

If you are interested in becoming a sound worker, you can start experimenting with sounds and effects on your computer at home. Listen to current games and try to recreate their sounds or work with a group of friends to create a brand new game that contains sound effects and music that you have come up with on your own.

The Internet is a great place to learn more about the computer and video game industry and sound careers. Online publications such as *Game Developer* (http://www.gdmag.com) will provide you with an overview of opportunities in the industry. You can also subscribe to the *Music4Games Newsletter* (http://www.music4games.net) to read reviews of current games and production tools, as well as interviews with those in the field. Check out http://www.audiogang.org, the site for the Game Audio Network Guild, which offers student membership. You also might want to read the online publication, *Breaking In: Preparing For Your Career in Games,* which is available at the International Game Developers Association's website, http://www.igda.org/breakingin. It offers an overview of sound careers, profiles of workers in the field, and other resources.

Another way to learn more about the field is to attend the annual Game Developers Conference. This will allow you to meet people in the business and other enthusiasts, see new games and technologies, and even attend workshops of interest to you. Of course, this event can be expensive, but if your funds are limited, you may want to work as a student volunteer, which enables you to pay much less. Visit http://www.gdconf.com for more information about this conference.

EMPLOYERS

Sound workers are employed by computer game companies and developers. Some sound professionals, especially composers and musicians, work on a freelance or project basis. Many positions in the computer and video game industry are located on the East and West Coasts and aspiring sound workers may have to relocate to these regions to find work in the industry. There are a significant number of game companies in Illinois, Texas, Maryland, and Massachusetts.

Sound workers have many opportunities for employment outside of the computer and video game industry. For example, sound designers with specialized training may work in the recording, music video, radio, and television industries. Composers can try to sell their work to music publishers, film and television production companies, recording companies, dance companies, musical theater producers, and advertising agencies. Musicians can work for religious organizations, orchestra, schools, clubs, restaurants, and cruise lines; at weddings; in opera and ballet productions; and on film, television, and radio.

STARTING OUT

Sound workers can learn more about jobs in the industry by visiting game company websites and sites that advertise job openings, such as Game Jobs (http://www.gamejobs.com) and Gamasutra (http://www. gamasutra.com). Many people attend the annual Game Developers Conference to network and learn more about internship and job opportunities. Aspiring composers and musicians usually break into the industry by creating a demo tape of their work and submitting it along with a resume to game companies. They might also create a website that features samples of their work for potential employers to review.

ADVANCEMENT

With experience, sound workers at software publishers can advance to the position of *music* or *audio director* and oversee the work of sound designers and other professionals. Others might start their own companies and provide services to game companies on a freelance basis. Advancement for composers and musicians often takes place on a highly personal level. As they become known for their artistic abilities, they may be asked to compose or perform music for more prestigious projects or companies. Some may become well-known composers and musicians in the film and television industries or in the fine arts.

EARNINGS

According to Gamasutra.com's *2003 Game Development Salary Survey,* sound workers with two years or less experience earned average annual salaries of $45,780. Those with two to five years of experience averaged $53,540, and those with six or more years of experience averaged $77,745. According to the International Game Developers Association, salaries for sound workers range from $45,000 to $130,000, with an average of $57,500 annually.

The American Federation of Musicians of the United States and Canada has created a pay scale for musicians and composers who perform or write music for computer and video games. The current agreement is based on a minimum three-hour session, intended use, the number of musicians or composers involved in the project, and the stage in game development, among other factors. Under this agreement, musicians and composers are paid the following flat fees for each three-hour session: $144 for games in development, $175 for a single-platform product (music or composition may not be used in game sequels or in other platforms), and $198 for a multiplatform project (music or composition may be used in game sequels and in other platforms).

Full-time sound workers receive typical fringe benefits such as paid vacation and sick days, health insurance, and the opportunity to participate in retirement savings plans. Freelance sound workers must pay for their own health insurance and other benefits.

WORK ENVIRONMENT

Sound designers work in recording studios that are usually air conditioned because of the sensitivity of the equipment. Studios may be loud or cramped, however, especially during recording sessions where many people are working in a small space. Some designers may be required to record off-site, at live concerts, for example, or other places where the recording is to take place.

The physical conditions of a composer's workplace can vary according to personal taste and what is affordable. Some work in expensive, state-of-the-art home studios, others in a bare room with an electric keyboard or a guitar. Musicians employed in the game industry may work in recording studios, home studios, or at concert halls and other venues.

OUTLOOK

Although the use of sound in computer and video games is growing in importance, sound workers still make up a very small portion of professionals in the game industry. As a result, competition for jobs in the game industry is very strong. Sound workers who have a combined knowledge of sound design and composition and/or musical abilities will have very good employment prospects over the next decade. The rarest breed of sound worker is the professional who has expertise in both sound and game programming. Demand for these specialized workers will be especially strong over the next decade.

FOR MORE INFORMATION

For information on union pay scales for musicians employed in the game industry, contact

American Federation of Musicians of the United States and Canada
1501 Broadway, Suite 600
New York, NY 10036
Tel: 212-869-1330
Email: info@afm.org
http://www.afm.org

For information on student membership and audio recording schools and courses, contact
Audio Engineering Society
60 East 42nd Street, Room 2520
New York, NY 10165-2520
Tel: 212-661-8528
http://www.aes.org

For information on membership and industry awards for sound workers, contact
Game Audio Network Guild
PO Box 1001
San Juan Capistrano, CA 92393
Email: info@audiogang.org
http://www.audiogang.org

For information on music careers, contact
MENC: The National Association for
   Music Education
1806 Robert Fulton Drive
Reston, VA 20191
Tel: 800-336-3768
http://www.menc.org

NASM is an organization of schools, colleges, and universities that provide music education. Visit the website for a listing of NASM-accredited institutions.
National Association of Schools
   of Music (NASM)
11250 Roger Bacon Drive, Suite 21
Reston, VA 20190
Tel: 703-437-0700
Email: info@arts-accredit.org
http://nasm.arts-accredit.org

For information on membership, contact
Society of Professional Audio Recording Services
9 Music Square South, Suite 222
Nashville, Tennessee 37203
Tel: 800-771-7727
Email: spars@spars.com
http://www.spars.com

For general information on the game industry, visit
Game Developer
CMP Media LLC
600 Harrison Street, 3rd Floor
San Francisco, CA 94107
http://www.gdmag.com

To read interviews with sound workers, listen to music from popular video games, and to subscribe to the newsletter, visit
Music4Games Newsletter
http://www.music4games.net

—— INTERVIEW ——

Kevin Manthei is an award-winning game, film, and television composer. He spoke with the editors of Careers in Focus: Computer & Video Dame Design *about his career.*

Q. How would you describe your musical style?
A. I compose music for film, television, and games. Although my style changes from project to project, it always keeps a cinematic feel. My music grows out of my love for film scores and the emotional impact those scores have on their films. My style is cinematic with orchestral and electronic flares incorporating and distilling the right emotion and mood for the right situation.

Q. What are your primary and secondary job duties as a game composer.
A. I generally am responsible for the entire musical underscore soundtrack for the projects I work on. The score could be purely synthetic (using my project studio to complete the score) to a fully live orchestral score using an orchestra. It's my job to see the project from start to finish and hire the appropriate people to help me along the way.

Q. How long does it take to score a typical game?
A. A typical game has anywhere from 35 minutes to 90 minutes of music. I have worked on games that need music in as little as a few weeks to games where I have been working on the project on and off for over a year. I am usually working on more than one project at a time and switch between them on a weekly basis. On the games that I work on over a yearly period, there are many months where I am not working on the project. I

typically write between two to four minutes of music a day when composing. A good week of compositional progress for me is about 10 minutes of finished score.

Q. Other than your own artistic abilities, what tools or equipment do you use to compose?

A. I work out of my custom-built studio that is a separate structure at my house. Inside my studio, I have many computers around me. I rely heavily on the equipment of my studio to allow me to realize, synthesize, and compose my musical scores. I have two Macintosh computers, one for my sequencing and recording, the other for my general business activities. I have five PCs running Gigastudio (a software-based sampler) as well as other soft synth programs. These computers along with some older Roland Samplers, Access Virus B, and other analog modeling synths all feed into my two Yamaha 02R digital mixers. I have a few outboard reverbs and effects units as well as a video card to digitize video projects. This is all complimented with a large library of custom and bought sounds.

Q. How did you train for this career?

A. I have a master's degree in music theory and composition from the University of Minnesota as well as a certificate in scoring for motion pictures and television from the University of Southern California. School, though, can only teach you so much. I learned so much from mentoring with and working for film and television composers who hired me to help them in various positions. It was from watching others and observing them in real-world situations that helped me put it all together.

Q. What was your first job in the field? What did you do?

A. My first game score was for a Viacom New Media project based on the children's film *The Indian in the Cupboard*. It was a great introduction to the world of video game composing for me. I was asked to write 10 or so pieces in various styles all relating to the film and the specific styles needed for the video game. After composing the score for the game and having great success with it, I was so impressed with the medium I switched my focus from finding work in the film and TV world to that of games.

Q. What are the most important personal and professional qualities for game composers?

A. One of the most important and hardest things to learn is that you are composing music for a director/producer and you need to please that person. You're being hired to create music for THEIR game. Because of this working relationship, you need to be flexible when it comes to their feedback and not take things personally. You need to separate the creative and artistic process of composing your music from the business side of composing music for others. Other important qualities include patience, being easy to work with, having no ego issues, and keeping your word with schedules. Finally, it doesn't hurt if you're a good composer as well!

Q. What are some of the pros and cons of your job?

A. Pros: I own my own business so I define my own hours of work. I can work on any project I choose. (A composer rarely turns down a good paying job!) I can work from home. I use the creative side of my brain. It's rewarding to hear your music on a film, TV show, or game and see it in its final form. Your income increases as your project load increases. I get to do what I love—writing music!

Cons: There is the pressure of performance—your music has to be good and there is no time for writer's block! If you say yes to every project, your schedule can be very busy. Long hours are common if you don't have the right resources and people to help you. It's a freelance business so there are no guarantees for your income or workload. You are at the mercy of your clients and their feedback. You can't control the approval process of the music. It's very competitive.

Q. What advice would you give young people who are interested in becoming game composers?

A. Follow your dreams, but be realistic about it. This is a business as well as a creative field. You need to master both sides in order to be successful. You can't be afraid to sell yourself. You need to invest in your future by having a state-of-the-art studio to create your music in. You need to understand the business, who to contact, how to get a job and the things you need to do once you have that job. Make steps every day of your life toward your dream. Wishing and dreaming without action will get you nowhere quickly.

Q. What are the next music-based trends in the game industry?

A. I think the music in games will continue to become more interactive. Music continues to be a vital part of games and you will see more and more people recognizing composers of game music and the importance of their contributions to game music and the music community at large.

Q. You have received considerable acclaim for your work in motion pictures and television. Is it common for game composers to work in these industries?

A. I split my time between the two mediums throughout the year. I see many composers who do an occasional game or game composers who do an occasional film or TV project. I think it's not as common to find someone who does both equally. But it's becoming more common for film composers to work in both mediums.

Q. What are the main differences (in terms of scoring) between the two industries?

A. Music for film and television is ruled by the action on the screen. The screen (show, video, and so forth) dictates and calls out to you to score it a certain way. Your music must fit the action of the scene of the film. The worst thing you can do is ignore the screen and write a piece exactly the way you would like it while ignoring all the specific cues and hits you need to focus on. Games, on the other hand, allow one to write a cue without the need for hitting specific actions within a scene. With games, you're scoring an emotional bed that spurs the player on, gives the right tone for the level, and helps the development team make their creative point. To further my point with an example: I am scoring a new animated show called *Xiaolin Showdown*. It's a kids Kung Fu show on WB Kids! with lots of action. When I score the action scenes for *Xiaolin Showdown,* my music is all over the place in terms of style, volume, tempo, and meters. This is because in order to score everything correctly, (dialogue, cuts, action), I need to really mix it up to score the scene. But if I were scoring the *Xiaolin Showdown* game, I would be free to let the ideas of the same TV action piece flourish. I would be able to compose freely without the confines of changing action of the scene. Melodies would not be interrupted and musical builds could last as long as I like. That's the challenge of both genres!

Technical Support Specialists

OVERVIEW

Technical support specialists in the computer and video game industry investigate and resolve problems in computer and video game functioning. They listen to customer complaints, walk customers through possible solutions, and write technical reports based on these events. Technical support specialists have different duties depending on whom they assist and what they fix. Regardless of specialty, all technical support specialists must be very knowledgeable about the products with which they work and be able to communicate effectively with users from different technical backgrounds. They must be patient with frustrated users and be able to perform well under stress. Technical support is basically like solving mysteries, so support specialists should enjoy the challenge of problem solving and have strong analytical thinking skills. There are approximately 507,000 computer support specialists employed in the United States.

HISTORY

The first major advances in modern computer technology were made during World War II. After the war, it was thought that the enormous size of computers, which easily took up the space of entire warehouses, would limit their use to huge government projects. The 1950 census, for example, was computer-processed.

The introduction of semiconductors to computer technology made possible smaller and less expensive computers. Businesses began adapting computers to their operations as early as 1954. Within 30 years, computers had revolutionized the way people work, play, and go shopping. Today, computers are everywhere, from businesses of all kinds to government agencies, charitable organizations, and private homes. Over the years, technology has continued to shrink computer size and increase speed at an unprecedented rate.

Technical support has been around since the development of the first computers for the simple reason that, like all machines, computers always experience problems at one time or another. The need for technical support specialists has been increasing since the job's inception. Several market phenomena explain this increase in demand for competent technical support specialists. First of all, as more and more companies enter the computer and video game hardware, software, and peripheral market, the intense competition to win customers has resulted in many companies offering free or reasonably priced technical support as part of the purchase package. A company uses its reputation and the availability of a technical support department to differentiate its products from those of other companies. The increase in the number of different companies in the market has also contributed to compatibility issues among the products of different makers of games for the many models of computers or video game consoles. These issues are usually resolved with a technical support specialist. Second, computer and video game consoles and personal computers have entered private homes in large numbers over the past decades, and the sheer quantity of users has risen so dramatically that more technical support specialists are needed to field their questions and complaints. Third, technological advances hit the marketplace in the form of a new processor or software application so quickly that quality assurance departments cannot possibly identify all the glitches in programming beforehand. Finally, given the great variety of computer equipment and software on the market, it is often difficult for users to reach a high proficiency level with each individual program. When they experience problems, often due to their own errors, users call on technical support to help them. The goal of many computer and video game companies is to release a product for sale that requires no technical support, so that the technical support department has nothing to do. Given the speed of development, however, this is not likely to occur anytime soon. Until it does, there will be a strong demand for technical support specialists.

THE JOB

Computer and video games can be played on several different platforms—such as personal computers (PCs), manufactured by many different companies, with many different technical configurations; video game consoles, like PlayStation, GameCube or Xbox; or on a handheld device, like a Game Boy. Many games have versions available for some or all platforms. Even if the games themselves were free of errors—which is unlikely—it is almost impossible to program a game to play flawlessly when the user's choice of platform introduces many variables that can't be taken into account when a game is initially designed. This is especially true with games created to play on PCs. Any game or platform that routinely frustrates the game player and doesn't offer any resolution is not going to be a viable competitor in the marketplace. Hence, the need for computer and video game technical support specialists was created. When game players experience problems with their computer and video game systems, they know they can look to technical support for help.

Technical support specialists are typically employed by the manufacturers of game platforms, by the studios that design games, and by the publishers of computer and video games. They investigate and resolve problems in the game or platform's functioning. They also create collections of technical support information that users can access to try to solve problems on their own. These collections can be accessed via the Internet, by having users search the collection for known issues with a particular product; or via the telephone, where users can access the information through a phone menu. Allowing game users an opportunity to solve the problem on their own saves both time and money for the gamer, the technical support specialist, and the company that employs the specialist. It also frees up the technical support specialist to handle more complex problems that cannot be solved as easily.

The jobs of technical support specialists vary according to whom they assist and what they fix. Some specialists help game users of one game or platform exclusively; others handle many games across several platforms. Specialists often work directly with game players themselves, who call or email the specialists when they experience problems. The technical support specialist carefully considers the game player's explanation of the precise nature of the problem and the action that seem to have caused it.

The initial goal is to isolate the source of the problem. If user error is the culprit, the technical support specialist explains possible solutions related to the problem in question, whether it is a graphics, audio, or performance issue. If the problem seems to lie in the hardware or software, the specialist asks the user to enter certain commands or take certain actions in order to see if the computer game makes the appropriate response. If it does not, the technical support specialist is closer to isolating the cause. The technical support specialist consults supervisors, game programmers, and others in order to outline the cause and possible solutions. Some companies have developed complex software that allows the technical support specialist to enter a description of the problem and wait for the computer to provide suggestions about what the game player should do. This helps improve response time. This is especially important for technical support specialists assisting players participating in online games.

Some technical support specialists who work for computer companies are mainly involved with solving problems whose cause has been determined to lie in the computer system's operating system, hardware, or software. They make exhaustive use of resources, such as colleagues or books, and try to solve the problem through a variety of methods, including program modifications and the replacement of certain hardware or software. It may become apparent that the problem does not lie with the product of the technical support specialist's company, but with the product of another hardware manufacturer or software company—especially when dealing with games that perform on the PC platform.

All technical support work must be well documented. Support specialists write detailed technical reports on every problem they work on. They try to tie together different problems on the same software, so programmers can make adjustments that address all of the issues. Record keeping is crucial because industry workers such as game designers, software programmers, and hardware engineers use technical support reports to revise current products and improve future ones. Some support specialists help write training manuals. They are often required to read trade magazines and company newsletters in order to keep up to date on their products and the field in general.

REQUIREMENTS

High School
A high school diploma is the minimum educational requirement for technical support specialists. Any technical courses you can take, such as computer science, schematic drawing, or electronics, can help you develop the logical and analytical thinking skills necessary to be successful in this field. Courses in math and science are also valuable for this reason. Since technical support specialists have to deal with both computer programmers on the one hand and computer users who may not know anything about computers on the other, you

Technical support specialists should have knowledge of computer and video games, the ability to solve problems, and excellent communication skills since they often deal with customer questions and complaints via the phone or by email. *(RF, Photodisc)*

should take English and speech classes to improve your communications skills, both verbal and written.

Postsecondary Training

Technical support is a field as old as computer technology itself, so it might seem odd that postsecondary programs in this field are not more common or standardized. The reason behind this situation is relatively simple: formal education curricula cannot keep up with the changes, nor can they provide specific training on individual products. Some large corporations might consider educational background, both as a way to weed out applicants and to insure a certain level of proficiency. Most major computer companies, however, look for energetic individuals who demonstrate a willingness and ability to learn new things quickly and who have general computer knowledge. These employers count on training new support specialists themselves.

Individuals interested in pursuing a job in this field should first determine what area of technical support appeals to them the most and then honestly assess their level of experience and knowledge. Large corporations often prefer to hire people with an associate's degree and some experience. They may also be impressed with commercial certification in a computer field, such as networking. However, if they are hiring from within the company, they will probably weigh experience more heavily than education when making a final decision.

Employed individuals looking for a career change may want to commit themselves to a program of self-study in order to be qualified for technical support positions. Many computer professionals learn a lot of what they know by playing around on computers, reading trade magazines, and talking with colleagues. Self-taught individuals should learn how to effectively demonstrate knowledge and proficiency on the job or during an interview. Besides self-training, employed individuals should investigate the tuition reimbursement programs offered by their company.

High school students with no experience should seriously consider earning an associate's degree in a computer-related technology. The degree shows the prospective employer that the applicant has attained a certain level of proficiency with computers and has the intellectual ability to learn technical processes, a promising sign for success on the job.

There are many computer technology programs that lead to an associate's degree. A specialization in personal computer support and administration is certainly applicable to technical support. Most computer professionals eventually need to go back to school to earn a bachelor's degree in order to keep themselves competitive in the job market and prepare themselves for promotion to other computer fields.

Certification or Licensing

Though certification is not an industry requirement, it is highly recommended. According to the Help Desk Institute, most individuals wishing to qualify to work in a support/help desk environment will need to obtain certification within a month of being on the job. A number of organizations offer several different types of certification. The Computing Technology Industry Association, for example, offers the "A+" certification for entry-level computer service technicians. The Help Desk Institute has training courses and offers a number of certifications for those working in support and help desk positions.

To become certified, you will need to pass a written test and in some cases may need a certain amount of work experience. Although going through the certification process is voluntary, becoming certified will most likely be to your advantage. It will show your commitment to the profession as well as your level of expertise. In addition, certification may qualify you for certain jobs and lead to new employment opportunities.

Other Requirements

To be a successful computer and video game technical support specialist, you should be patient, enjoy challenges of problem solving, and think logically. You should work well under stress and demonstrate effective communication skills. You should also enjoy playing computer and video games. You will need to learn about the products you are supporting and the other various hardware and software products associated with them, as you will be spending a great deal of time helping gamers troubleshoot problems with a game and the platform on which they are playing the game, such as a PC, handheld device, or video game console. Working in a field that changes rapidly, you should be naturally curious and enthusiastic about learning new technologies as they are developed.

EXPLORING

If you are interested in becoming a technical support specialist, you should try to interview a worker employed in the field. You can ask about the most common questions and complaints they receive, and how they handle them. Computer hardware or software companies that offer technical support service, especially those in the game industry, are good places to contact.

You should also start working and playing on computers as much as possible; many working computer professionals became computer hobbyists at a very young age. You can surf the Internet, read computer magazines, and join school or community computer clubs.

You might also attend a computer technology course at a local technical/vocational school. This would give you hands-on exposure to typical technical support training. In addition, take advantage of any problems you experience with your own hardware or software—call technical support, paying close attention to how the support specialist handles the call and asking as many questions as the specialist has time to answer.

EMPLOYERS

Technical support specialists in the computer and video game industry work for game development studios, computer and video game publishers, or manufacturers of the various computer and video game platforms. In addition, some smaller studios and companies outsource their customer support to companies that do nothing but handle customer support for a variety of products. Technical support specialist jobs are plentiful in areas where clusters of computer companies are located, such as northern California and Seattle, Washington. Outside of the computer and video game industry, technical support specialists work for other computer hardware and software companies, as well as in the information systems departments of large corporations and government agencies. There are approximately 507,000 technical support specialists employed in the United States.

STARTING OUT

Most technical support positions are considered entry level. They are found mainly in larger game development studios, computer and video game publishers, or manufacturers of the various computer and video game platforms. Individuals interested in obtaining a job in this field should scan the classified ads for openings in local businesses and may want to work with an employment agency for help finding out about opportunities. Since many job openings are publicized by word of mouth, it is also very important to speak with as many working computer professionals as possible. They tend to be aware of job openings before anyone else and may be able to offer a recommendation to the hiring committee.

If students of computer technology are seeking a position in technical support, they should work closely with their school's placement office. Many employers inform placement offices at nearby schools of openings before ads are run in the newspaper. In addition, placement office staffs are generally very helpful with resume and interviewing techniques.

ADVANCEMENT

Computer and video game technical support specialists who demonstrate leadership skills and a strong aptitude for the work may be promoted to supervisory positions within technical support departments. Supervisors are responsible for the more complicated problems that arise, as well as for some administrative duties such as scheduling, interviewing, and job assignments. There are limited opportunities for technical support specialists to be promoted into additional managerial positions. Doing so would require additional education in business, but would probably also depend on the individual's advanced computer knowledge and knowledge of the company's products.

EARNINGS

Median annual earnings for technical support specialists employed by software publishers were $42,870 in 2002, according to the U.S. Department of Labor. Technical support specialists employed in all industries had salaries that ranged from less than $23,060 to $67,550 or more in 2002. Those who have more education, responsibility, and expertise have the potential to earn much more.

Most technical support specialists work for companies that offer a full range of benefits, including health insurance, paid vacation, and sick leave. Smaller service or start-up companies may hire support specialists on a contractual basis.

WORK ENVIRONMENT

Technical support specialists work in comfortable business environments. They generally work regular, 40-hour weeks. For certain products, however, they may be asked to work evenings or weekends or at least be on call during those times in case of emergencies. If they work for service companies, they may be required to travel to clients' sites and log overtime hours.

Technical support work can be stressful, since specialists often deal with frustrated users who may be difficult to work with. Communication problems with people who are less technically qualified may also be a source of frustration. Patience and understanding are essential for handling these problems.

Technical support specialists are expected to work quickly and efficiently and be able to perform under pressure. The ability to do this requires thorough technical expertise and keen analytical ability.

OUTLOOK

The U.S. Department of Labor predicts that employment for technical support specialist will grow faster than the average through 2012. Each time a new computer and video game product is released on the market or another platform is introduced, there will be problems, whether from user error or technical difficulty, especially with games played on the PC platform. Therefore, there will always be a need for technical support specialists to solve the problems. Since technology changes so rapidly, it is very important for these professionals to keep up to date on advances. They should read trade magazines, surf the Internet, and talk with colleagues in order to know what is happening in the field.

Since some companies stop offering technical support on old products or applications after a designated time, the key is to be technically flexible. This is important for another reason as well. Even thought there is much growth predicted for this career, that does not necessarily equate with more jobs being available in the United States. There is some concern with the growing trend of companies exporting their technical support services to other countries where labor costs are much lower. Technical support specialists interested in working for computer companies should therefore consider living in areas in which many such companies are clustered. In this way, it will be easier to find another job if necessary.

FOR MORE INFORMATION

For information on internships, scholarships, student membership, and the student magazine Crossroads, *contact*
Association for Computing Machinery
1515 Broadway
New York, NY 10036
Tel: 800-342-6626
http://www.acm.org

For information on certification, contact
Computing Technology Industry Association
1815 South Meyers Road, Suite 300
Oakbrook Terrace, IL 60181-5228
Tel: 630-678-8300
http://www.comptia.org

For computer and video game industry information, contact
Entertainment Software Association
1211 Connecticut Avenue, NW, #600
Washington, DC 20036
Email: esa@theesa.com
http://www.theesa.com

Gamasutra
600 Harrison Street, 3rd Floor
San Francisco, CA 94107
Tel: 415-947-6206
http://www.gamasutra.com

For more information on this organization's training courses and certification, contact
Help Desk Institute
6385 Corporate Drive, Suite 301
Colorado Springs, CO 80919
Tel: 800-248-5667
Email: support@thinkhdi.com
http://www.thinkhdi.com

For information on careers, scholarships, student membership, and the student newsletter looking.forward, contact
IEEE Computer Society
1730 Massachusetts Avenue, NW
Washington, DC 20036-1992
Tel: 202-371-0101
http://www.computer.org

For career advice and industry information, contact
International Game Developers Association
600 Harrison Street, 6th Floor
San Francisco, CA 94107
Tel: 415-947-6235
Email: info@igda.org
http://www.igda.org

Video Game Testers

QUICK FACTS

School Subjects
Art
Computer science
Mathematics

Personal Skills
Mechanical/manipulative
Technical/scientific

Work Environment
Primarily indoors
Primarily one location

Minimum Education Level
Bachelor's degree

Salary Range
$16,245 to $27,061 to
$67,419+

Certification or Licensing
Voluntary

Outlook
Faster than the average

DOT
N/A

GOE
N/A

NOC
N/A

O*NET-SOC
N/A

OVERVIEW

Video game testers examine new or modified video game applications to evaluate whether or not they perform at the desired level. Testers also verify that different tasks and levels within a game function properly and progress in a consistent manner. Their work entails trying to find glitches in games and sometimes crashing the game completely. Testers keep very close track of the combinations they enter so that they can replicate the situation in order to remedy it. Testers also offer opinions on the user-friendliness of video and computer games. Any problems they find or suggestions they have are reported in detail both verbally and in writing to supervisors.

According to the Interactive Digital Software Association, approximately 145 million people play video and computer games. In other words, 60 percent of all Americans age six and older help to make the gaming industry a success.

HISTORY

Over the years, technology has continued to shrink computer size and increase speed at an unprecedented rate. The video game industry first emerged in the 1970s. Early engineers included Ralph Baer and Steve Russell. Magnavox first manufactured Russell's TV game, *Odyssey,* in 1972.

Atari and Sega were the prominent manufacturers of video games throughout the 1970s and 1980s. Nintendo gained popularity in the mid-1980s, and continues to be a dominant player in the industry. Although gaming is a relatively new industry, companies such as Magnavox and Nintendo are more than a century old.

The field of testing and quality assurance has changed with the advent of automated testing tools. There will always be a need for video game testers, however, since they, not a computer, are best suited to judge a game from a user's point of view.

THE JOB

The primary responsibilities of video game testers are game testing and report writing. Testers work with all sorts of games, including handheld electronic devices, computer programs, and traditional video games, which are played on the television screen. As technology advances, testers are responsible for games on more compact electronic devices, such as mobile telephones and palm-sized electronic organizers, as well as online games.

Before video game manufacturers can introduce a game to the consumer market, they must run extensive tests on its quality and effectiveness. Failing to do so thoroughly can be very expensive, resulting in poor sales when games are defective or do not perform well. Video and computer games require extremely detailed technical testing.

Games to be tested arrive in the testing department after programmers and software engineers have finished the initial version. Each game is assigned a specific number of tests, and the video game testers go to work. To test a game, testers play it over and over again for hours, trying to make moves quickly or slowly to "crash" it. A program crashes if it completely stops functioning due to, among other things, an inability to process incoming commands. Testers spend the majority of their time identifying smaller glitches or discrepancies in games, which are known as "bugs."

Video game testers must clearly report any bugs that they find in a game. They keep detailed records of the hours logged working on individual programs. These are called bug reports. Bug reports are based on the tester's observations about how well the game performed in different situations. Testers must always imagine how typical, nontechnical users would judge it. Video game testers can also make suggestions about design improvements.

Prior to being employed in this field, it is important for potential video game testers to carefully observe how different types of people play games. This will help to ensure that suggestions and evaluations reflect more than just personal bias.

In addition, testers verify that video games perform in accordance with designer specifications and user requirements. This includes checking not only the game's functionality (how it will work), but also its network performance (how it will work with other products), installation (how to put it in), and configuration (how it is set up).

Once video game testers make sure that the correct tests are run and the reports written, they send the game back to the programmers for revisions and correction. Some testers have direct contact with the programmers. After evaluating a product, they might meet with programmers to describe the problems they encountered and suggest ways for solving glitches. Others report solely to a game testing coordinator or supervisor.

The goal is to make the video games and computer programs more efficient, user-friendly, fun, and visually exciting. Testers keep track of the precise combinations of controller movements, keystrokes, and mouse clicks that made the program err or crash. These records must be very precise because they enable supervisors and programmers to replicate the problem. Then they can better isolate its source and begin to design a solution.

Video game testers work closely with a team of development professionals. *Computer and video game developers* and *designers* create and develop new games. They delegate responsibilities to *artists, writers,* and *audio engineers* who work together to produce the developer's desired vision of each game. These professionals creatively collaborate their ideas of style and flow to make each game a polished and engaging finished project. *Programmers* have to reproduce the bugs before they fix them. *Producers* keep the video game's progress on schedule and within budget.

REQUIREMENTS

High School
Interested in becoming a video game tester? If so, then take as many computer classes as possible to become familiar with how to effectively operate computer software and hardware. Math and science courses are very helpful for teaching the necessary analytical skills. English and speech classes will help you improve your verbal and written communication skills, which are also essential to the success of video game testers.

Postsecondary Training
It is debatable whether or not a bachelor's degree is necessary to become a video game tester. Many companies require a bachelor's degree in computer science, while others prefer people who come from the business sector who have a small amount of computer experience because they best match the technical level of the software's

typical users. Courses in computer science and psychology are beneficial. Some companies require job seekers to submit a short writing sample when applying for a testing position.

If testers are interested in advancement, however, a bachelor's degree is almost certainly a requirement. Few universities or colleges offer courses on video game testing. As a result, most companies offer in-house training on how to test their particular games. A few specialized schools, like The Academy of Game Entertainment Technology, offer courses such as Introduction to Computer Gaming, Game Testing, and Test Management. A very small number of schools, including DigiPen Institute of Technology, exist solely to train digital entertainment developers.

Certification or Licensing

As the gaming and information technology industries become more competitive, it is increasingly important for video game testers to demonstrate professionalism in the workplace. Some game development companies encourage testers to earn computer technician certificates. Such certificates can be obtained at community colleges and technical institutes, as well as four-year colleges and universities. Also, the Quality Assurance Institute offers the certified software tester, certified software quality analyst, and certified software project manager designations to applicants who pass an examination and satisfy other requirements.

Other Requirements

Video game testers need strong verbal and written communication skills. They also must show a proficiency in critical and analytical thinking and be able to critique a product diplomatically. Video game testers should have an eye for detail, be focused, and have a lot of enthusiasm because sometimes the work is monotonous and repetitive. Testers should definitely enjoy the challenge of breaking the system.

Some companies recommend that testers have some programming skills in languages such as C, C++, SQL, or Visual Basic. The most important thing is that testers understand the gaming business and the testing tools with which they are working. Video game testers should also be creative problem solvers.

EXPLORING

Students interested in video game testing and other computer jobs should gain wide exposure to computer systems and video games of

Game Player Stats

- Sixty percent of Americans age six and older play computer and video games.

- The average game player is 29 years old.

- The average game purchaser is 36 years old.

- More than 90 percent of games are purchased by people over the age of 18.

- Women make up 41 percent of computer and video game players.

Source: Entertainment Software Association

all kinds. ST Labs/Data Dimensions Inc. offers the following advice: Become a power user. Get a computer at home, borrow a friend's, or check out the computer lab at your school. First, work on becoming comfortable using Windows programs and learn how to operate all of the computer, including the hardware, thoroughly. Look for bugs in your software at home and practice writing them up.

Secondly, play as many video and computer games as you can. Get good at all different types of games. Learn the differences between games and become familiar with all commands, tasks, and shortcuts.

Keep up with emerging technologies. If you cannot get much hands-on experience, read about the industry. Join a computer group or society. Read books on testing and familiarize yourself with methodology, terminology, the development cycle, and where testing fits in. Subscribe to newsletters or magazines that are related to video game testing, programming, animation, and game design, such as *Game Developer* (http://www.gdmag.com) and *Video Business* (http://www.videobusiness.com). Get involved with online newsgroups that deal with the subject—Gamasutra (http://www.gamasutra.com) is one to try.

If you live in an area where numerous video game development companies are located, like the Silicon Valley in northern California, for example, you might be able to secure a part-time or summer job as a video game tester. An internship with a game development company or any computer-related internship will be a helpful learning experience.

If possible, save up to attend the Game Developers Conference when you are a sophomore or junior in high school. This is a great chance to network with industry and make yourself known. In addition, investigate the possibility of spending an afternoon with a video game tester to find out what a typical day is like for him or her.

EMPLOYERS

Video game testers are employed by computer and video game manufacturers. The *Occupational Outlook Quarterly* refers to games as the Wild West of the computer industry, meaning that no two gaming companies are organized in the same way. There are approximately 219,000 people employed in the computer and video game industry.

Opportunities are best in large cities and suburbs where business and industry are active. Many testers work for video game manufacturers, a cluster of which are located in Silicon Valley, in northern California. There is also a concentration of software manufacturers in Boston, Chicago, and Atlanta.

STARTING OUT

Positions in the field of video game testing can be obtained several different ways. Many universities and colleges host computer job fairs on campus throughout the year that include representatives from several hardware and software companies. Internships and summer jobs with such corporations are always beneficial and provide experience that will give you the edge over your competition. General computer job fairs are also held throughout the year in larger cities. Some job openings are advertised in newspapers. There are also many online career sites listed on the World Wide Web that post job openings, salary surveys, and current employment trends.

ADVANCEMENT

Video game testers are considered entry-level positions in most companies. After acquiring experience and industry knowledge, testers might advance to any number of professions within the gaming industry. Project managers, game test coordinators, game designers, developers, and programmers are among the possibilities.

EARNINGS

The U.S. Department of Labor does not publish data specifically on video game testers. It reports that all inspectors and testers had median annual earnings of $27,061 in 2002. Salaries ranged from less than $16,245 to more than $49,005.

According to Salary.com, software quality assurance workers earned salaries that ranged from less than $48,402 to $67,419 in 2004. Most testers receive paid vacation and sick leave and are eligible to participate in group insurance and retirement benefit plans.

WORK ENVIRONMENT

Video game testers work in game development studios. They play games for a living, and this work can be very fun and entertaining. However, the work is also generally repetitive and even monotonous. If a game is being tested, for example, a tester may have to play it for hours until it finally crashes, if at all. This might seem like great fun, but most testers agree that even the newest, most exciting game loses its appeal after several hours. This aspect of the job proves to be very frustrating and boring for some individuals.

Video game developers may put in long hours in order to meet deadlines. Their work hours usually include nights or weekends. During the final stages before a game goes into mass production and packaging, however, testers are frequently called on to work overtime.

Since video game testing work involves keeping very detailed records, the job can also be stressful. For example, if a tester works on a game for several hours, he or she must be able to recall at any moment the last few moves or keystrokes entered in case the program crashes. This requires long periods of concentration, which can be tiring.

Meeting with supervisors, programmers, and developers to discuss ideas for the games can be intellectually stimulating. At these times, testers should feel at ease communicating with superiors. On the other end, testers who field customer complaints on the telephone may be forced to bear the brunt of customer dissatisfaction, an almost certain source of stress. The video game industry is always changing, so testers should be prepared to work for many companies throughout their careers.

OUTLOOK

The number of positions in the gaming industry is expected to grow faster than the average through 2012. According to the Entertainment Software Association (ESA), computer and video game sales were $7 billion in 2003, and are expected to maintain steady growth.

Companies in the gaming industry continue to gain popularity and respect. *Fortune* magazine named Electronic Arts one of the 100 Best Companies to Work For in 2003.

The push toward premarket perfection will also help to keep the video game testing profession strong. To stay competitive, companies are refining their procedures to ever higher levels. One thing is for sure—the video game industry is here to stay. According to the ESA, 53 percent of the most frequent computer and video game players expect to be playing games as much or more 10 years from now as they do today.

FOR MORE INFORMATION

For information on scholarships, student memberships, and the student newsletter looking.forward, *contact*
IEEE Computer Society
1730 Massachusetts Avenue, NW
Washington, DC 20036-1992
Tel: 202-371-0101
http://www.computer.org

For industry information, contact the following associations:
Entertainment Software Association
1211 Connecticut Avenue, NW, #600
Washington, DC 20036
Email: esa@theesa.com
http://www.theesa.com

Software & Information Industry Association
1090 Vermont Ave, NW, Sixth Floor
Washington, DC 20005-4095
Tel: 202-289-7442
http://www.siia.net

For information on careers in the computer and game development industry, contact
International Game Developers Association
600 Harrison Street, 6th Floor
San Francisco, CA 94107
Tel: 415-947-6235
Email: info@igda.org
http://www.igda.org

For information on certification, contact
Quality Assurance Institute
7575 Dr. Phillips Boulevard, Suite 350
Orlando, FL 32819
Tel: 407-363-1111
http://www.qaiusa.com

To check out video game reviews, learn about classic games, and read about school programs in this industry, visit the following websites:
GameDev.Net
http://www.gamedev.net

Video Game Yellow Pages
http://www.vgyellowpages.com

For information on software testing, contact
Software Testing Institute
http://www.softwaretestinginstitute.com

Webmasters

OVERVIEW

Webmasters design, implement, and maintain Internet websites for businesses of all types, including computer and video game developers. webmasters working in the gaming industry create, operate, and maintain sites that provide free games, tips and tricks on mastering games, or help promote, sell, and support games. Regardless of what type of site webmasters operate, they should have working knowledge of network configurations, interface, graphic design, software development, business, writing, marketing, and project management. Because the function of a webmaster encompasses so many different responsibilities, the position may be shared by a team of individuals.

HISTORY

The World Wide Web was the brainchild of physicist Tim Berners-Lee (born in 1955), who developed a way to organize information in a more logical fashion by using hypertext to link portions of documents to one another. Although Berners-Lee formed his idea of the Web in 1989, it was another four years before the first Web browser (Mosaic) made it possible for people to navigate the Web simply. Businesses quickly realized the commercial potential of the Web and soon developed their own websites.

Today, the Internet houses thousands of for-profit sites that aim to promote and sell products such as computer and video games. Yahoo, Amazon, AOL, and Microsoft all offer sites that allow users to purchase games online. Other sites exist simply for entertainment. These sites, such as Miniclip.com and Download.com, offer free games, videos, and other media for free download. All these websites need skilled webmasters to create, run, and maintain them.

THE JOB

Because the idea of designing and maintaining a website is relatively new, there is no complete, definitive job description for webmasters. Many of their job responsibilities depend on the goals and needs of the particular company for which they work. There are, however, some basic duties that are common to almost all webmasters.

Webmasters, specifically site managers, first secure space on the Web for the site they are developing. This is done by contracting with an Internet service provider. The provider serves as a sort of storage facility for the organization's online information, usually charging a set monthly fee for a specified amount of megabyte space. The webmaster may also be responsible for establishing a URL (Uniform Resource Locator) for the website he or she is developing. The URL serves as the site's online "address" and must be registered with InterNIC, the Web URL registration service.

Webmasters are then responsible for developing the actual website for their business. In some cases, this may involve actually writing the text content of the pages. More commonly, however, the webmaster is given the text to be used and is merely responsible for programming it in such a way that it can be displayed on a Web page. In larger companies, webmasters specialize in content, adaptation, and presentation of data.

In order for text to be displayed on a Web page, it must be formatted using HyperText Markup Language (HTML). HTML is a system of coding text so that the computer that is "reading" it knows how to display it. For example, text could be coded to be a certain size or color or to be italicized or boldface. Paragraphs, line breaks, alignment, and margins are other examples of text attributes that must be coded in HTML.

Although it is less and less common, some webmasters code text manually, by actually typing the various commands into the body of the text. This method is time consuming, however, and mistakes are easily made. More often, webmasters use a software program that automatically codes text. Some word processing programs, such as WordPerfect, even offer HTML options.

For any website, especially those selling products such as computer or video games, webmasters must be concerned with the visual elements of the site. They may use various colors, background patterns, images, tables, or charts. These graphic elements can come from image files already on the Web, game clip art files, or images scanned into the computer with an electronic scanner. In the case of a game developer, the webmaster may work with the company's marketing specialist or department to develop a page that is not only informative and interesting, but will also help boost online product sales.

Some websites have several directories or "layers." That is, an organization may have several Web pages, organized in a sort of "tree," with its home page connected, via hypertext links, to other pages, which may in turn be linked to other pages. The webmaster is responsible for organizing the pages in such a way that a visitor can easily browse through them and find what he or she is looking for. Such webmasters are called *programmers* and *developers;* they are also responsible for creating Web tools and special Web functionality.

For webmasters who work for companies that have several different websites, one responsibility may be making sure that the "style" or appearance of all the pages is the same. This is often referred to as "house style." In large organizations, where many different departments may be developing and maintaining their own pages, it is especially important that the webmaster monitor these pages to ensure consistency and conformity to the organization's requirements. Webmasters must carefully edit, proofread, and check the appearance of every page.

Besides designing and setting up websites, most webmasters are charged with maintaining and updating existing sites. Most sites contain information that changes regularly. Some change daily or even hourly. Depending on the webmaster's site, a good deal of time is spent updating and remodeling Web pages. Webmasters are also responsible for ensuring that the hyperlinks contained within the site lead to the sites they should. Since it is common for links to change or become obsolete, the webmaster usually performs a link check every few weeks.

Other job duties vary, depending on the employer and the position. Most webmasters are responsible for receiving and answering email messages from visitors to the organization's website. Many gaming sites offer online forums where users can post messages about games they have played. The webmaster receives all these messages and must make sure they are suitable for posting online. Some webmasters keep logs and create reports on when and how often their pages are visited and by whom. Depending on the company, websites count anywhere from 300 to 1.4 billion visits, or "hits," a month. Some create and maintain order forms or online "shopping carts" that allow visitors to the website to purchase computer or video games for home use. Finally, webmasters may be responsible for developing and adhering to a budget for their departments.

REQUIREMENTS

High School

High school students who are interested in becoming a webmaster should take as many computer science classes as they can. Mathematics classes are also helpful. Finally, because writing skills are important in this career, English classes are good choices. To run a site centered on gaming, you should be passionate about gaming yourself. While in high school, experiment with various games and platforms and read about the history of game development and older technologies that have been used and replaced. This sense of history will help you understand where the industry stands now and help you relate to other game players.

Postsecondary Training

A number of community colleges, colleges, and universities offer classes and certificate programs for webmasters, but there is no standard educational path or requirement for becoming a webmaster. While many have bachelor's degrees in computer science, information systems, or computer programming, liberal arts degrees, such as English, are not uncommon. There are also webmasters who have degrees in engineering, mathematics, and marketing.

Certification or Licensing

There is strong debate within the industry regarding certification. Some, mostly corporate chief executive officers, favor certification. They view certification as a way to gauge an employee's skill and Web mastery expertise. Others argue, however, that it is nearly impossible to test knowledge of technology that is constantly changing and improving. Despite the split of opinion, webmaster certification programs are available at many colleges, universities, and technical schools throughout the United States. Programs vary in length, anywhere from three weeks to nine months or more. Topics covered include client/server technology, Web development, programs, and software and hardware. The International webmasters Association and the World Organization of webmasters also offer voluntary certification programs.

Online Gaming Stats

- More than 186 million console games were sold in the United States; more than 23 percent of these games were Web-enabled for online play.

- The most popular types of online games were puzzle/board/trivia/card games (54.7 percent), action/sports games (21.1 percent), Shockwave/Flash games (13.1 percent), and persistent multiplayer universe games (7.8 percent).

- Forty-three percent of online game players played for one or more hours per week—an increase of 12 percent from 2002.

Source: Entertainment Software Association, 2003

Should webmasters be certified? Though it's currently not a prerequisite for employment, certification can only enhance a candidate's chance at landing a webmaster position.

What most webmasters have in common is a strong knowledge of computer technology. Most people who enter this field are already well versed in computer operating systems, programming languages, computer graphics, and Internet standards. When considering candidates for the position of webmaster, employers usually require at least two years of experience with World Wide Web technologies. In some cases, employers require that candidates already have experience in designing and maintaining websites. It is, in fact, most common for someone to move into the position of webmaster from another computer-related job in the same organization.

Other Requirements
Webmasters, especially those working for game developers or hosting sites, should be creative. It is important for a Web page to be well designed in order to attract attention and solicit excitement and response. Good writing skills and an aptitude for marketing are also excellent qualities for anyone considering a career in website design and operation.

EXPLORING

One of the easiest ways to learn about what a webmaster does is to spend time "surfing" on the World Wide Web. By examining a variety of websites to see how they look and operate—especially those that focus on computer and video games—you can begin to get a feel for what goes into a home page.

An even better way to explore this career is to design your own personal Web page. For example, if you are passionate about gaming, create a site centered on computer and video games. You could create a ranking of your top 10 games. Many Internet servers offer their users the option of designing and maintaining a personal Web page for a very low fee. A personal page can contain virtually anything that you want to include, from snapshots of friends to audio files of favorite music to hypertext links to other favorite sites.

EMPLOYERS

According to *Interactive Week,* the majority of webmasters working today are full-time employees. Many of those working in the computer and video game industry work for game developers. Electronic Arts is the largest independent publisher of interactive entertainment. Other large corporations such as Microsoft and Disney have also opened interactive entertainment departments. The majority of these companies are located in Washington, New York, Illinois, and California, though game developers of all sizes are located around the world.

Some webmasters may also work as freelancers or operate their own Web design businesses, such as those that post "cheats" (tricks) or lists of the most popular games.

STARTING OUT

Most webmasters working for game developers move into the position from another computer-related position within the company. Since most large organizations already use computers for various functions, they may employ a person or several people to serve as computer "specialists." If these organizations decide to develop their own websites, they frequently assign the task to one of these employees who is already experienced with the computer system. Often, the person who ultimately becomes an organization's webmaster at first just takes on the job in addition to his or her other, already established duties.

Another way that individuals find jobs in this field is through online postings of job openings. Many companies post webmaster position openings online because the candidates they hope to attract are very likely to use the Internet for a job search. Therefore, the prospective webmaster should use the World Wide Web to check job-related newsgroups.

ADVANCEMENT

Experienced webmasters employed by a large game developer may be able to advance to the position of *chief Web officer*. These workers supervise a team of webmasters and are responsible for every aspect of a company's presence on the Web. Others might advance by starting their own business, designing websites for gaming companies on a contract basis rather than working exclusively for one organization.

Opportunities for webmasters of the future are endless due to the continuing development of online technology. As understanding and use of the World Wide Web increase, there may be new or expanded job duties for individuals with expertise in this field. People working today as webmasters may be required in a few years to perform jobs that don't even exist yet.

EARNINGS

According to Salary.com, the average salary for webmasters in 2004 was $61,797. Salaries ranged from $52,016 to $74,348. However, many webmasters move into the position from another position within their company or have taken on the task in addition to other duties. These employees are often paid approximately the same salary they were already making.

According to the National Association of Colleges and Employers, the starting salary for graduates with a bachelor's degree in computer science was $47,109 in 2003; in computer programming, $45,346; and in information sciences and systems, $38,282.

Depending on their employer, webmasters may receive a benefits package in addition to salary. A typical benefits package would include paid vacations and holidays, medical insurance, and perhaps a pension plan.

WORK ENVIRONMENT

Although much of the webmaster's day may be spent alone, it is nonetheless important that he or she be able to communicate and work well with others. Depending on their employer, the webmaster may have periodic meetings with graphic designers, marketing specialists, writers, or other professionals who have input into the website development. In many larger organizations, there is a team of webmasters rather than just one. Although each team member works alone on his or her own specific duties, the members may meet frequently to discuss and coordinate their activities.

Because technology changes so rapidly, the gaming industry will continue to change and become more and more technical in nature. Webmasters must be able to keep up with this development. To do this, they spend time reading and learning about technological advancements in online communication and game development. They may be continually working with new computer software or hardware that run newer, better, and faster games. Their actual job responsibilities may even change, as the capabilities of both their employer and the World Wide Web itself expand. It is important that these employees be flexible and willing to learn and grow with the technology that drives the computer and video game industry and, as a result, their own work.

Because they don't deal with the general public, most webmasters are allowed to wear fairly casual attire and to work in a relaxed atmosphere. In most cases, the job calls for standard working hours, although there may be times when overtime is required.

OUTLOOK

According to the U.S. Department of Labor, the field of computer systems design and related services is projected to be one of the fastest growing industries for the next decade. As a result, the employment rate of webmasters and other computer specialists is expected to grow faster than the average rate for all occupations through the next decade.

There can be no doubt that computer, and specifically online, technology will continue its rapid growth for the next several years. Likewise, then, the number of computer-related jobs, including that of webmaster, should also increase. The study by *Interactive Week* finds the field to be currently male-dominated, with men making up 74.9 percent of workers. However, there are great opportunities for women in computer science.

Companies that design, develop, and sell computer and video games will always have an online presence. As a result, these companies will always need experts to design and run their websites. Most companies now view websites as important and necessary business and marketing tools. Growth will be largest for *Internet content developers,* webmasters who are responsible for the information displayed on a website, and chief Web officers.

One thing to keep in mind, however, is that when technology advances extremely rapidly, it tends to make old methods of doing things obsolete. If current trends continue, the responsibilities of the webmaster will be carried out by a group or department instead of a single employee, in order to keep up with the demands of the position. It is possible that in the next few years, changes in technology will make the websites we are now familiar with a thing of the past. Another possibility is that, like desktop publishing, user-friendly software programs will make website design so easy and efficient that it no longer requires an "expert" to do it well. Webmasters who are concerned with job security should be willing to continue learning and using the very latest developments in technology, so that they are prepared to move into the future of online communication, whatever it may be.

FOR MORE INFORMATION

For industry information, contact
Entertainment Software Association
1211 Connecticut Avenue, NW, #600
Washington, DC 20036
Email: esa@theesa.com
http://www.theesa.com

For career advice and industry information, contact
**International Game Developers
    Association**
600 Harrison Street, 6th Floor
San Francisco, CA 94107
Tel: 415-947-6235
Email: info@igda.org
http://www.igda.org

*For information on training and certification programs, contact the
following organizations:*
International Webmasters Association
119 East Union Street, Suite F
Pasadena, CA 91103
Tel: 626-449-3709
http://www.iwanet.org

World Organization of Webmasters
9580 Oak Avenue Parkway, Suite 7-177
Folsom, CA 95630
Tel: 916-608-1597
Email: info@joinwow.org
http://www.joinwow.org

Writers and Editors

OVERVIEW

Writers and *editors* employed in the computer and video game industry write articles, reviews, and books about computer and video games, platforms, companies, and the industry as a whole. Other writers and editors work for game companies and developers and write and edit content for games, user manuals, websites, and in other areas. Some writers and editors may be full-time salaried workers, but many are employed on a freelance basis. There are approximately 319,000 writers and editors employed in the United States. A small percentage of this group are employed in the computer and video game industry.

HISTORY

Ever since the dawn of the commercial game industry in the 1970s, writers and editors have been employed by game companies and developers to write and edit technical documentation, advertising copy, and any other text that was required to produce and sell video games and consoles. But it wasn't until the creation of more complex and multifaceted games in the mid-to-late 1990s that writers and editors became an integral part of the creation of actual video and computer games. In addition to handling technical and advertising responsibilities at game companies, today's writers and editors create the plot, story lines, dialogue (known as "barks"), and voice-overs for computer and video games. As games companies continue to compete for market share in this highly competitive industry, these professionals will be increasingly relied upon to give each game an extra edge.

QUICK FACTS

School Subjects
Computer science
English

Personal Skills
Communication/ideas
Technical/scientific

Work Environment
Primarily indoors
Primarily one location

Minimum Education Level
Bachelor's degree

Salary Range
$24,010 to $45,000 to
$80,900+

Certification or Licensing
None available

Outlook
About as fast as the average

DOT
131, 132

GOE
01.01.01, 11.08.02, 11.08.01

NOC
5121, 5122

O*NET-SOC
27-3022.00, 27-3041.00,
27-3042.00, 27-3043.00

Although video games became immensely popular by the late 1970s, the first magazine devoted entirely to gaming wasn't founded until 1981. *Electronic Games* had its origins in a columnist named Bill Kunkel—a professional musician and comic book scriptwriter, wrote for *Video* magazine in the late 1970s. *Electronic Games* was the industry leader until it ceased publication in 1985. Despite continued growth in the industry in the 1980s and early 1990s, there were relatively few magazines specifically devoted to computer and video gaming. The emergence of the Internet, improvements in game technology, and steady increases in game sales created strong interest in games, new technology, and the industry as a whole. Many publications were founded to serve the needs of industry professionals, as well as the interests of people who played the games. Today, writers and editors are employed by countless print and online magazines that focus on the everchanging computer and video game industry.

THE JOB

Writers and editors employed in the computer and video game industry can be divided into two major areas: those who are employed by the media to write articles, feature stories, reviews, or books about products, trends, or the industry in general and those who are employed by game companies and developers to write and edit content for computer and video games and user manuals.

Print and online publications. Writers and editors who are employed by computer and video game publications perform many of the same duties as writers and editors employed in other industries. The only difference is that they focus on the computer and video game industry.

Writers express, edit, and interpret ideas and facts about the game industry in written form for books, magazines, trade journals, newspapers, and company newsletters. They might review a popular online game, write an article about the delay in the launch of a much-anticipated new game platform, or interview a famous game designer or studio head. Many computer and video game publications are only available online. Writing for this medium is much different than writing for print. Online writers must be able to write in a style that provides information while also engaging the reader's interest. They must pay special attention to the tone and length of an article. Few readers will scroll through screen after screen of text. While online writers do not need to be computer geniuses, they do need to know what computer and Internet tools can make their articles more interesting. Frequently, online writers incorporate highlighted key words, lists, pop-up boxes or windows, and hyper-text links in their articles. These items make the articles visually appealing and easy to read. Writers must have a love of games and expertise about the industry.

Editors ensure that text provided by writers is suitable in content, format, and style for the intended audiences—whether they are employed by a magazine geared toward teen gamers or publications for game industry executives. They might have specialized titles—such as game review editor, hardware editor, platform/console editor, or news editor—based on the types of writing they edit.

Some writers and editors are full-time salaried employees of publishers, while many others may work on a freelance basis. As free-lancer, writers or editors run their own businesses. They may get an assignment from a company to write a particular article, or they may write an article and then attempt to sell it to a company for publication. Freelancers also need business skills to keep track of their financial accounts and market their work.

Computer and video game companies and developers. Writers and editors employed by this branch of the game industry have a variety of job opportunities. *Scriptwriters,* also known as *screenwriters,* create the plot, story lines, dialogue, and voice-overs for computer and video games. Unlike movie or television scriptwriting, writing a video game does not typically involve a linear plot, but rather a plot that contains multiple and expanding branches and many different outcomes depending on the skill and actions of the game player. Scriptwriters who focus on interrelated dialogue are called *interactive conversation writers.* Scriptwriters must be keenly aware of every possibility that can occur in a game and write dialogue and plot lines that match these possibilities. They need to understand basic character development, context setting, and backstory and setting design. Scriptwriters must also have a strong knowledge of the background and history of the game for which they are writing content. For example, a scriptwriter creating content for a game set in Europe during World War II would need to have knowledge of (or be able to research) British and American military lingo; the weapons, vehicles, and other equipment used during the war; the history of Allies and Axis countries during that time span; and other facts about this conflict. Scriptwriters work closely with game designers to ensure that their writing and the technical pacing of the game are in sync. Unless they also have experience as game programmers, scriptwriters do not usually participate in the initial planning stages of a game, but are hired on a contract basis after the game idea has been approved for creation.

Technical writers and editors employed in the game industry prepare a wide variety of documents and materials. They might write and edit content for user guides; training manuals; package copy and game summaries; installation instructions for software, hardware, or related materials; and Help and Technical Support sections on company websites. Others may write and edit consumer publications published by game companies such as Nintendo. Computer and video game companies and developers also employ *copywriters,* who write advertising copy for computer and video game packaging, company websites, and print and radio and television advertisements.

One drawback to working as a writer or editor in the game industry is that many publishers and game companies are not well established, and thus job security is minimal. However, for those interested in being on the cutting edge of the game industry and having their writing available to millions, this field is the right place to be.

REQUIREMENTS

High School

If you are interested in becoming a writer or editor, take English (including creative writing), literature, foreign languages, general science, social studies, computer science, and typing classes while in high school. The ability to type is almost a requisite for all positions in the communications field, as is familiarity with computers.

Editors and writers must be expert communicators, so you should excel in English if you wish to work in these careers. You must learn to write extremely well, since you will be correcting and even rewriting the work of others. If they are offered at your school, take elective classes in writing or editing, such as creative writing, journalism, and business communications.

Postsecondary Training

Most writing and editing jobs require a college education. Many employers prefer that you have a broad liberal arts background or majors in English, literature, history, philosophy, or one of the social sciences. Other employers desire communications or journalism training in college. Game manual writers might be required to have an advanced degree in computer science, engineering, or a related discipline.

In addition to formal course work, most employers look for practical writing and editing experience. If you have served on high school or college newspapers, yearbooks, or literary magazines, you will make a better candidate, as well as if you have worked for small community newspapers or radio stations, even in an unpaid position. Many computer and video game companies, book publishers, magazines, and newspapers have summer internship programs that provide valuable training if you want to learn about the publishing business. Interns do many simple tasks, such as running errands and answering phones, but some may be asked to perform research, conduct interviews, or even write or edit some minor pieces.

Other Requirements

Writers and editors should be creative and able to express ideas clearly, have broad general knowledge, be skilled in research techniques, and be knowledgeable about computers and the gaming industry. You must have the desire and initiative to keep up on new technology and the changes that are constantly taking place in the game industry. Other assets include curiosity, persistence, initiative, resourcefulness, and a good memory.

You must be detail oriented to succeed as a writer or an editor. You must also be patient, since you may have to spend hours synthesizing information into the written word or turning a few pages of near-gibberish or technical jargon into powerful, elegant English. If you are the kind of person who can't sit still, you probably will not succeed in these careers. To be a good writer or editor, you must be a self-starter who is not afraid to make decisions. You must be good not only at identifying problems but also at solving them, so you must be creative.

EXPLORING

If you are interested in becoming a game writer or editor, you should play as many computer and video games as possible. Become familiar with the various gaming companies, platforms, and trends in the business. Pick your favorite (or least favorite) game and write a review of its best and worst features. Consider the game's audio, art design, animation, playability, and other factors when writing your review. If you're interested in becoming a scriptwriter, you should focus on the strengths or weaknesses of a game's plot, character, dialogue, and voice overs.

Another way to learn more about writing and editing careers and the game industry in general is to read publications about the field. There are many online magazines that feature reviews and articles about computer and video games. Some popular publications include *Game Developer* (http://www.gdmag.com), *Animation World* (http://mag.awn.com), GameZone Online (http://www.gamezone.com), *Computer Graphics World* (http://www.cgw.com), *GameInformer* (http://www.gameinformer.com), and *VideoGameNews* (http://videogamenews.com). You also might want to read the online publication *Breaking In: Preparing For Your Career in Games,* which is available at the International Game Developers Association's website, http://www.igda.org/breakingin. It offers an overview of game industry careers (including writer), profiles of workers in the field, and other resources.

As a high school or college student, you can test your interest and aptitude in the fields of writing and editing by working as a reporter or writer on school newspapers, yearbooks, and literary magazines. If you cannot work for the school paper, try to land a part-time job on a local newspaper or newsletter. If that doesn't work, you might want to publish your own newsletter or create your own website devoted to gaming. This will give you a forum for your writing, allow you to interact with other gamers, and learn more about the publishing industry.

Many online game publications solicit reviews and short articles from young people. Most of these do not pay or only offer a small payment or game tokens, but they are excellent ways to hone your writing and have your opinions read by a larger audience. Reputable sites often will provide clips of published work which you can use to help you develop your portfolio.

Information on writing and editing as a career may also be obtained by visiting local newspapers and game publishers and interviewing some of the people who work there. Career conferences and other guidance programs frequently include speakers on the entire field of communications from local or national organizations.

EMPLOYERS

Writers and editors in the game industry work for publishing companies of various sizes. Others work for independent game development studios and manufacturers of the various computer and video game platforms. These companies are usually located on the East and West Coasts—although computer and video game companies can also be found in Illinois, Texas, and other states. Major entertainment software publishers include Electronic Arts, Nintendo of America, Activision, Atari, Sony, Vivendi Universal, THQ, Take 2 Interactive, Microsoft, and Konami of America.

Approximately 319,000 writers and editors are employed in the United States. Only a small percentage of this group is employed in the computer and video game industry.

STARTING OUT

You can apply for employment directly to game companies or publishing companies with gaming publications. Be sure to research these companies first to learn more about their products or editorial focus. Don't send your resume and writing samples to every employer that has a job listing. Look for work settings that match your interests and abilities.

There are many websites that have job listings for writers and editors. These include Game Jobs (http://www.gamejobs.com) and Gamasutra (http://www.gamasutra.com). Many people also attend the annual Game Developers Conference to network and learn more about internship and job opportunities.

Your college career services office and journalism or communications department should be able to give you help with your job search. In addition, contacts that you make during an internship or summer job may provide employment leads.

ADVANCEMENT

Most writers and editors employed by game publishers find their first jobs as editorial or production assistants. Advancement may be more rapid at small publications, where beginners learn by doing a little bit of everything and may be given writing or editing tasks immediately. At large publications, duties are usually more compartmentalized. Assistants in entry-level positions are assigned such tasks as research, fact checking, and copyrighting, but it generally takes much longer to advance to full-scale writing or editing duties. A typical advancement path for editors might include the following steps: editorial/production assistant, copy editor, senior copy editor, project editor, first assistant editor, managing editor, and editor in chief.

Scriptwriters can advance by being assigned to work on more important games or by taking on management responsibilities for a project. Since they work so closely with game developers, many also gain enough experience to work in this career.

As technical writers and editors gain experience, they move into more challenging and responsible positions. At first, they may work on simple documents or are assigned to work on sections of a document. As they demonstrate their proficiency and skills, they are given more complex assignments and are responsible for more activities. Technical writers and editors with several years of experience may move into project management positions. As project managers, they are responsible for the entire document development and production processes. Technical writers and editors who show good project management skills, leadership abilities, and good interpersonal skills may become supervisors or managers. Both technical writers and editors can move into senior writer and senior editor positions. These positions involve increased responsibilities and may include supervising other workers.

Freelance or self-employed writers and editors earn advancement in the form of larger fees as they gain exposure and establish their reputations.

EARNINGS

The U.S. Department of Labor does not publish salary data for writers and editors employed in the game industry. It reports that all writers earned salaries that ranged from less than $42,970 to more than $85,140 in 2002. Earnings of technical writers are somewhat higher. In 2002, technical writers earned salaries that ranged from less than $30,270 to $80,900 or more. Median annual earnings for technical writers were $50,580.

The U.S. Department of Labor reports that the median annual earnings for all editors were $41,170 in 2002. Salaries ranged from $24,010 or less to more than $76,620.

In addition to their salaries, many writers and editors earn income from freelance work. Freelance earnings vary widely. Full-time established freelance writers and editors may earn up to $75,000 a year. Part-time writers may be paid on a per-review or per-article basis. These one-time fees may range from as little as $5 to $50 for a game review to $50 to $300 or more for a full-length article.

Typical benefits may be available for full-time salaried employees including sick leave, vacation pay, and health, life, and disability insurance. Retirement plans may also be available, and some companies may match employees' contributions. Some companies may also offer stock-option plans.

Freelance writers and editors do not receive benefits and are responsible for their own medical, disability, and life insurance. They do not receive vacation pay, and when they aren't working, they aren't generating income. Retirement plans must also be self-funded and self-directed.

WORK ENVIRONMENT

Working conditions vary for writers and editors. Although the work-week usually runs 35 to 40 hours, many writers and editors work overtime.

Physical surroundings range from comfortable private offices to noisy, crowded newsrooms filled with other workers typing and talking on the telephone. Some writers must confine their research to the library or telephone interviews, but others may travel to other cities or countries or to local sites, such as game companies, game conferences, or other business settings.

OUTLOOK

There will always be a need for writers and editors in the computer and video game industry, whether they write or edit game scripts, advertising copy, and game manuals or write or edit articles or books about games and the industry. Opportunities will be especially strong for writers and editors with online publishing experience. Employment will also be good for scriptwriters and technical writers and editors as the number of computer and video games produced each year continues to increase. The U.S. Department of Labor predicts that employment for writers and editors employed in all industries will grow about as fast as the average through 2012.

FOR MORE INFORMATION

For industry information, contact the following associations:

Entertainment Software Association
1211 Connecticut Avenue, NW, #600
Washington, DC 20036
Email: esa@theesa.com
http://www.theesa.com

Software & Information Industry Association
1090 Vermont Ave, NW, Sixth Floor
Washington, DC 20005-4095
Tel: 202-289-7442
http://www.siia.net

For information on careers in the computer and game development industry, contact
International Game Developers Association
600 Harrison Street, 6th Floor
San Francisco, CA 94107
Tel: 415-947-6235
Email: info@igda.org
http://www.igda.org

For information on awards and internships, contact
Society of Professional Journalists
Eugene S. Pulliam National Journalism Center
3909 North Meridian Street
Indianapolis, IN 46208
Tel: 317-927-8000
Email: questions@spj.org
http://www.spj.org

For additional information regarding online writing and journalism, check out the following websites:
Online News Association
http://www.onlinenewsassociation.org

Visit the following website for comprehensive information on journalism careers, summer programs, and college journalism programs.
High School Journalism
http://www.highschooljournalism.org

Index

New York City, New York 43, 53, 74, 85
New York Times 76
Nintendo Software Technology
   entertainment software publisher 38, 48, 49,
      99, 111, 154, 178
   employer 11–12, 83, 94, 112, 131, 176
NPD Group 32
Nuremburg trials 74

O

object builder. *See* 3D object specialist
Occupational Outlook Handbook
   earnings
      hardware engineers 62
      software store employees 127
   employers
      video game testers 159
   employment outlook
      hardware engineers 63
      package designers 97
   job growth 3
Odyssey, The 14, 120, 154
online gaming 62, 163, 167
Online News Association 182

P

packaging designers 90–98
Pac-Man 4, 25, 29
PageMaker 5
Parberry, Ian 29
PASCAL 48
patents 67
PDA. *See* Personal Digital Assistant
persistent worlds 26
Personal Digital Assistant (PDA) 1, 52
Peyser, Seymour 74
Phillips Nizer Benjamin Krim and Ballon 74
Photoshop 5
Planetdeusex.com 122
PlayStation 1, 58, 62, 99, 145
Pokemon 49
Pong
   creation of 14, 25, 37, 48, 79
   designing 29
   early video game 4, 99
producers 99–106, 156
production assistants 101
production team 27
project supervisors (marketing research analysts)
   81
project team leaders 113
psychologists (marketing research analysts) 81

Q

QA programmers 39
*Q*bert* 4
Quality Assurance Institute 157, 162

R

Radio Shack 120
Ramones 132
Redmond, Washington 11, 28
research assistants (marketing research
   analysts) 86

retail sales workers. *See* software store employees
Revolution Software 34
Roland Samplers 140
royalties 31
Russell, Steve 13–14, 24, 37, 47, 154

S

Salary.com 160, 169
sales research 80
San Francisco, California 43, 53
Santa Monica, California 74, 75
screenwriters 175, 179
scriptwriters 175
Sears 120
Seattle, Washington, 43, 53, 70, 149
Sega 38, 48, 99, 154
self-employment
   graphics programmers 53
   package designers 94
   sound workers 131, 136, 137, 141
   writers and editors 180
senior producers 100
senior programmers 39, 53
shopping carts 166
SIGGRAPH. *See* Special Interest Group on
   Computer Graphics
Silicon Valley (California) 70, 158, 159
Sims, The 28, 48
skeleton 17
Sloan Career Cornerstone Center 64
Smalltalk 48
Society of Professional Audio Recording Services
   138
Society of Professional Journalists 182
Software and Information Industry Association
   88, 116, 161, 181
software engineers 107–119
Software Etc. 125
software managers 113
software publishers 30
software store employees 120–129
Software Testing Institute 162
Sony
   employer 83, 94, 112, 178
   entertainment software publisher 111
   new game systems 38, 48, 99
   Online Entertainment 1
sound designers 131
sound effects designers 132–133
sound engineers 131, 156
sound library 132
sound programmers. *See* audio programmers
sound workers 130–142
Space Invaders 25
Spacewar 13, 24, 37, 47, 79
Special Interest Group on Computer Graphics
   (SIGGRAPH) 19, 20, 50, 52, 56
Spherion Jobs 31
SQL 157
ST Labs/Data Dimensions Inc. 158
Star Trek 25
statisticians (marketing research analysts) 81
Stores 129